Communicating

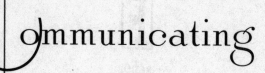

with the

Dead

Linda Georgian

A FIRESIDE BOOK
Published by Simon & Schuster
New York London Toronto
Sydney Tokyo Singapore

FIRESIDE
Rockefeller Center
1230 Avenue of the Americas
New York, NY 10020

FIRESIDE and colophon are registered trademarks
of Simon & Schuster Inc.

Designed by Jennifer Ann Daddio

Manufactured in the United States of America

1 3 5 7 9 10 8 6 4 2

Library of Congress Cataloging-in-Publication Data

Georgian, Linda M.
Communicating with the dead / Linda Georgian.
p. cm.
Includes bibliographical references.
1. Spiritualism. 2. Georgian, Linda. I. Title.
BF1261.2.G45   1995
133.9—dc20   95-23806 CIP

ISBN 0-684-81088-3

To all who have "lost" someone special and who are grieving, I dedicate this book to bridge the gap between this dimension and the other, to offer comfort and the awareness that those living here can have a continued relationship with those who are only a dimension away.

Acknowledgments

I have been fortunate to be guided by some incredible people who do not fall neatly into the categories of colleagues, friends, or family. The three overlap, and I feel truly blessed by that.

Thank you to my Simon & Schuster family: Jack Romanos; Carolyn Reidy; Mark Gompertz; my editor, Sydny Miner (who, as always, made this whole process such a pleasure); Marilyn Abraham; Sue Fleming; Chris Lloreda; Lisa Dolin; and Rachel Rader.

A very special thank you to my agent and friend, Lynn Franklin, whose guidance and support mean so much to me, and to Nina L. Diamond, writer and editor, who brought this book out of my head and onto the printed page.

For their continued love and encouragement, my heartfelt thanks to my eternal friends Marge and Irv Cowan; my friends John Vlack and Debbie Pierce; my dedicated assistants, Kelly Eastwood and Ann Rinella; my business manager, Peter Green; SSA publicist Christen Eckles in Los Angeles; Curtis Skoda for his invaluable help; and Adrienne Moore, for her promotional assistance.

Special thanks to my infomercial co-host, Dionne Warwick, whose light never ceases; to my dear friends Jacqueline Janssen, Jill Hearn, Dr. Don and Deborah Carrow, John Nero, Jon Dasher, and David Goodman.

Pam Johnson, Erica Rauzin, D.L., Gladys Seymour Davis, James Redfield, Dannion Brinkley, Michele Tumlin, Maureen Murray, Marilyn Sunderman, Matthew Glassman, Bob Diamond, Timolin Cole, Dr. Deborah Mash, Shirley Farmer, Carol and Aaron Friedman, Lil and Mickey Cohen, Laura Caster, Rob and Kathryn Cowdery, Gary Wilson, Amy Phillips, Mindi Rudan, Edie and Marty Bruckner, Debbie Einhorn, and Jonathan Ellis contributed wisdom and support that made this book possible.

Thank you to my family for a lifetime of love and encouragement—my sister, Sandra Post; my niece Patti Post; my nephew, Daniel Silagy, and his family; and, of course, special hugs go to my dog, Smarty.

To those who have passed on and continue to guide me from spirit, who have educated me on their spiritual mission in the afterlife, my love to my stepfather, Howard Simmons; the Reverend Jewell Williams, who was instrumental in opening me up to my abilities and continues to teach me; to my closest friend in the afterlife, Bob Yarbrough, who's always around; to my friend Pam Rosen, my Aunt Jenny, Aunt Helen, Aunt Rosie, and all of my other family who live on in spirit.

Thank you also to Abe, Bill C., Sally and Zada, whose

Acknowledgments

guidance, encouragement, and pep talks from the afterlife kept everything on track.

Most important, I thank my mother, Marie Georgian Simmons; and my father, Anthony Georgian, whose eternal love from the afterlife surrounds me, guides me, and teaches me every day.

Finally, my very special thanks to the thousands from all over the world who have shared their experiences with me for the last twenty-five years. And to those who have so generously shared your experiences in this book I offer my deepest gratitude.

Contents

Introduction

Recently, I heard about a pretty remarkable group of women. Although their story begins in sadness and grief, it ends in the kind of joy that spiritual experiences can bring to your life.

This group was not formally created, but rather evolved slowly as one friend after another in a prosperous suburb of a New England city suddenly became a widow.

First there were two women in their sixties who began to spend more time together after their husbands passed away. Having someone else around who understood so clearly their particular kind of grief was so soothing to both of them. They'd go out to dinner, take in a movie or a play, keep each other updated on their children and grandchildren. Of course, they'd also talk about their late husbands. Soon, a third woman, also newly widowed, began to join them on social occasions, then a fourth. Eventually, there were six women in the group, and when the talk turned to their husbands, they not only shared their grief and their happy family stories, they also shared a few mysteries, ones they were afraid that so-called outsiders would never *believe*, let alone understand.

"It had been nearly two years since my husband died and I felt ready to date," one woman (we'll call Anne) confided to her friends. "But, I also felt guilty, because we'd been married for more than forty years and even *looking* at another man felt like cheating. So, one morning while I was making the bed, I decided I'd have a little talk with him, even though he was dead, and explain that it was time for me to accept a date. And to ask his permission to move on, too, I guess."

She tucked the top sheet in, fluffed the pillows, and put on the bedspread, all the while talking aloud to her dead husband, telling him that although she would always love him, she would soon be open to meeting new suitors.

"I asked him if it would be okay," Anne continued. "And I asked him to send me a sign. Then I left the house to run some errands. When I came back about an hour later, I went into our bedroom (I still thought of it as *ours*), put my purse on the dresser, looked into the mirror, and saw the reflection of the bed. *The mattress had slid halfway off the box spring!* It never even occurred to me that someone might have broken into the house, though I did check around later and found nothing missing, no doors or windows open. I knew right away that *he* moved the mattress, somehow, as his way of saying, 'Hey, this is still *my* bed and I don't want you in it with anyone else!'"

The sight of the mattress hanging half off the bed made her laugh, and somehow reassured her of her husband's presence and of his enduring love. Not long after, she did go on her first date, and eventually she remarried.

Anne was the first to tell this kind of story to the group, but none of them seemed shocked. Each one of them had had a similar experience. Each one had been in some kind of contact with her late husband, and one by one they shared their stories.

Not only did it help Anne and her friends to have had a communication from the afterlife, it helped to be able to share that story with other people who cared and understood. It eased the grief for all the women as each told her story that night, and it continued to help them deal with their losses as the days, months, and years passed.

We all experience loss and grief. Even if someone lives to be 120, it's never the right time to lose a loved one.

My aim in writing this book is to provide comfort, hope, and the *truth:* that life *does* go on after we die. A different dimension of life, to be sure, but we do go on.

I wrote this book as a guide through some of the basic concepts and techniques for those who want to become more receptive to interdimensional communication, to the possibilities of every level of consciousness and the doors that open from these levels. You'll learn how natural this process is from those who have shared their experiences here among these pages.

While we can't bring the dead back to life as we know

it, we can relieve the grief and loss we feel. We can replace those feelings with joy and happiness when we understand where our loved ones have gone, what their purpose now becomes, and how we can continue to communicate with them and they can continue to communicate with us.

According to many well-respected national polls, the vast majority of Americans believe in life after death. A recent Gallup poll puts the figure at 66 percent. *Harper's* magazine noted in 1994 that 56 percent of Americans believe that there is baseball in heaven—perhaps some were shown a glimpse of a World Series in the afterlife dimension when the strike did away with the earthbound plane's national championship in the fall of 1994. Researchers at Eastern Virginia Medical School last year found that 40 percent of those surveyed felt that they kept in touch with those who had passed on. The University of Chicago's National Opinion Research Council reports that 42 percent of Americans believe that they have been in contact with someone who has died.

It's clear that many of us have had afterlife communications, and even the most skeptical persons become more open to the concept when it enters into their experience.

What kind of existence is there in the afterlife dimension? Every culture and time-honored tradition, and even physical science, has its own description. I've found that many common threads wind through these beliefs and reports.

In Part One of this book, we'll explore some of these afterlife concepts and descriptions as expressed by Eastern and Western philosophies, the world's major religions, and the teachings of native peoples.

In Part Two, we will look at the practical applications of afterlife communication, why people communicate with those who have passed on and why those who have passed on want to communicate with us. You'll see how to initiate, respond to, and interpret these communications. To illustrate all of these points dozens of people from around the country share their experiences, and I discuss a few of my own.

Much is being written today about the Near Death Experience (NDE) and the Out of Body Experience (OBE). Reports from those having such experiences and the research in these areas are the most exciting source of current information on the afterlife dimension. This information is quite easily accessed by many whose bodies die and are then revived, and by those having a mind-body separation while in a deeper level of consciousness, which frees one's soul to travel.

Throughout the book we'll look at the afterlife information gleaned from both of these phenomena.

My study of spirituality and the abilities that I have been blessed with that go beyond my five senses have always been central to my life and its purpose, dating back to my early childhood.

Communicating with those in the afterlife has always seemed as natural to me as having a relationship with my family and friends who are still living and breathing in the flesh. I credit my mother with creating that loving, spiritually enriching atmosphere in our home while I was growing up and with continuing to inspire me right up until her death a few years ago.

Those who have read my book *Your Guardian Angels*

have already met my mother via the printed page. For those who haven't, allow me to introduce Marie Georgian Simmons.

As a practicing Catholic, my mother definitely had her traditional side. She had her rosary and candles, religious figurines, and mass on Sunday. But she also had a very basic spirituality that she did not believe was at odds with any organized religion. She believed in and communicated with angels. She had the ability to heal people with her hands. She had highly advanced intuitive—psychic—gifts. And she kept in touch regularly with those close to her who had died.

She looked at all of her abilities as gifts from God, gifts that she said her father (whom I didn't know because he had already passed on) had also possessed. From early childhood on, it became clear that I was the next person in the family to have been blessed this way. My father had strong religious beliefs, but he never talked about them or about spirituality. My older sister, Sandra, has a spiritual side, but has not had the intense experiences or abilities that my mother and I have had.

Over the years, my mother would tell me how her late parents and her brothers and sisters would visit her in her dreams. My grandmother would be cooking, my grandfather gardening, and both would give my mother advice in her dreams. In one dream, my mother sat by a lake and fished with her late brother. When my father passed on he visited with her on one particular occasion as spirit. He sat on the edge of her bed, and it was as if he were there with the full weight of his former body—she felt the weight as he sat on the bed and she saw the bed squish down as if someone were sitting on that spot.

I was raised in Cleveland, where my father, Anthony, was the greenkeeper for the city of Cleveland's golf courses. We were a typical middle-class Italian family, and both of my parents gave us plenty of love and support. I enjoyed a whirlwind of academic, athletic, and social activities, and won both academic and athletic awards.

By the time I was twelve, my psychic and spiritual abilities were also in full bloom. But no one outside my family knew that the high school girl who was winning English, French, history, soccer, field hockey, track and field, softball, golf, and baton-twirling awards, the vivacious runner-up in the Miss Teenage Cleveland pageant, was just as gifted at reading minds, and was receiving guidance from angels and those who were no longer breathing.

Only when I entered college did I share my beliefs and abilities with friends. Of course they were delighted at how practical this could be for them, and I was asked for plenty of advice. I was always happy to help, and even happier that my intuition was so accurate, a gift from God, as I would explain to my friends.

I graduated from Ohio University in 1968 with a bachelor of science degree in education and moved with my family to Fort Lauderdale, Florida. Later that year, my father died of leukemia at only fifty-eight, and naturally I became even closer to my mother.

Eventually, my mother and I made a pact: whoever died first would communicate with the other.

Like any young professional, I was eager to begin

working. I had a personal spiritual quest to attend to, but I had my career as a physical education teacher to launch into as well.

I received a master of science in learning disabilities at the Florida Institute of Technology. Following a lifelong interest in holistic health, I wrote my thesis on "The Nutritional Approach to Learning Disabilities."

My studies and career were progressing nicely, but I felt an odd restlessness. So many of my spiritual questions were unanswered. So, I did what the young and curious often do—I quit my job, packed up, and took off not only to "find myself" but to find out what role spirituality played in the world and how I could integrate it further into my life.

After a year of traveling through the Orient, learning about Eastern philosophy, I returned to Fort Lauderdale in the summer of 1971 with even more questions than I had had when I left. I had, however, made one concrete decision: I knew that I wanted to continue teaching, focusing on holistic living. I also knew I wanted to explore my intuitive gifts further. I was already clairvoyant, could see and interpret auras, and could feel a divine presence in my life. One morning I was given another gift: clairaudience, the ability to *hear* spiritual or psychic messages. I had prayed for that, and I believe I inherited that ability from my mother as well as it being a gift from God or the Higher Power. Suddenly I felt as if I had an open phone line to the spiritual realm.

Now everyone and everything could talk to me. I started thinking about everyone I knew who had passed away and requested to speak with them. Sometimes I'd get an angelic message, like reaching a spiritual voice mail: "The spirit you've requested can't return your call at the moment, but we'll pass your message along and he (or she) will get back to you."

When I heard from those who'd passed into the afterlife they had plenty to say. It was as if I were their public relations representative. They wanted me to tell their loved ones that they were okay, that they would be guiding them, and that they missed them, too.

After about two months of this, I felt more of a balance about my new clairaudient ability. I had to adjust to this new world of hearing spiritual messages. I wondered, Will I be hearing things constantly? Soon, I found that, like a telephone, the line wasn't open all the time. It was open when you picked up the phone to make a call and when you answered the ring. Like the phone, my spiritual buzzer didn't go off twenty-four hours a day, thank God! I also realized that my reception was limited: I'd get only information that was understandable to me. I didn't go into any kind of trance or become a channel for people to speak through me. I simply received information.

"It's so beautiful here," I heard. "Tell them I love them. There are angels and other spiritual beings here, training and schools."

Sometimes the messages might get more specific, with personal information for those here on earth, and more detail about what the afterlife is like. (In Chapter Two you'll read in great detail about some of the afterlife descriptions I've received.)

My mother passed away a few years ago. I was never closer to anyone else in my life and I felt that loss very deeply. But I also remembered our pact, and *knew* with all my heart and soul that although she had left the world as we know it, had left *this* dimension, she was still very much around. I knew she would contact me. I knew that our relationship would continue. She did, and it has.

The first time I asked for my mother after she passed on, she responded: "I can help you more from this side than I could when I was alive."

She has been true to her word.

Because of what she—and every other person who passes on—has learned in the afterlife, her guidance and wisdom have been, and continue to be, as valuable as God's guidance. I will share some specific instances with you later in this book, but in general let me say that her guidance touches all areas of my life, personal and professional. When she's around, I can literally *feel* her energy in the room, and in my own being. Many people who have had afterlife communication have reported those same feelings to me.

In my travels, at lectures and media appearances, everyone is eager to talk about afterlife communication: How does it happen? How do I ask for help? How do I recognize it when it comes? Where's the proof? I've been asked a million questions, and I hope that when you've finished reading this book you'll feel that you've received some helpful answers. I don't have all the answers, of course. No one does. At least not while we're in the human state. It's once we've passed on that our *real* education begins.

As it is written in the Buddhist classic *The Tibetan Book of the Dead*:

Introduction

Thine own consciousness, shining, void, and inseparable from the Great Body of Radiance, hath no birth, nor death, and is the Immutable Light.

PART ONE

Travels

of the

Soul

Our modern disbelief in anything but the physical aspects of life has limited investigation and development of some of our transcendental capacities.

JAMES REDFIELD

CHAPTER ONE

The Cultural,
Philosophical,
and Scientific Soul

While human beings often pay great
attention to the differences between our
many cultures, religions, and philosophies, we really do have much more in
common than we assume at first glance.
Our differences lie in the ways in which
we *express* the basic themes and questions about life and death; in the legends
and myths; the celebrations, rituals, and
man-made laws we rely on to try to
understand, interpret, and live with nature's mysteries.

Would you be surprised to learn
that the Orthodox Jew in Tel Aviv shares
many of the same basic spiritual beliefs
about the soul and the afterlife as the
Huna in Hawaii and the oriental philoso-

phies of Taoists, Buddhists, and Hindus across the globe?

Would you be shocked to know that the physicist in Boston studies the same energy principles as the Chinese mystics who have learned to master *chi* energy?

Have you ever wondered how continued human evolution affects what we call our spirituality? How the ability to perceive the world spiritually or intuitively, to go beyond our five senses and tap into higher dimensions is a function of the vibrational frequency of the energy that invests all human beings? Indeed, it is the very same energy we share with everything in the universe.

We've come to understand that science and spirituality are simply two different languages that seek to describe the same phenomena. Concepts of respect, harmony, and living the mysteries of nature are replacing the old paradigms of fear and control. We no longer dismiss the validity of an idea or explanation simply because we cannot yet fully explain it to everyone's satisfaction.

We are finally rediscovering the fact that we were created to be spiritual explorers.

The Hawaiian mystic, or shaman, is called the *kahuna*, which means "keeper of the secret," and I was about to meet with one. The year was 1970, and I was spending a month in the Hawaiian islands before a yearlong stay in Japan that would continue my spiritual education with immersion in Eastern philosophy, healing, and mysticism.

Walking up the path to the *kahuna's* gate, I thought of what I knew about shamans. Revered wise men and women of native peoples, they were, and still are, highly trained while also being uniquely blessed by gifts of nature, and of the spirit. Shamans are the bridge between the spirit world and the world of our five senses. They serve as the link between their people and the deeper levels of universal consciousness. They teach and they heal. They are mystics, and often serve as medicine men or women.

Shamans have the ability to be one with all life, be it animal, vegetable, mineral, or nonphysical spirit. They routinely communicate with all spiritual states, including the afterlife, and embody an ancient tradition of guidance by those who have passed on, placing particular emphasis on the spirits of their ancestors.

My companions and I were told that we should come to the gate at the edge of the jungle clearing that the *kahuna* called home. There was no bell and no telephone. Not to worry, we were told, the shaman will sense your presence and send someone out to fetch you.

We stood amid the lush and vibrant green trees and plants and waited. I wondered if we'd end up standing there all day. Within a few minutes we heard footsteps through a jungle path, and one of the *kahuna's* assistants appeared, opened the gate, and let us in. He guided us through the jungle on the side of the mountain on the island of Oahu, Hawaii's most popular tourist destination. But we were far from the crowded beaches and hotels of Honolulu. Walking through the jungle, we were in the Oahu that nature had created: pristine, alive, unaltered by man.

In a clearing we came upon a shack. Chickens roamed freely in and around the small, rustic homestead. There was no electricity and the shack didn't even have four enclosed walls. The home had an open design, and the wooden walls only half enclosed the it. The floor was made of rough-hewn boards. A wooden bowl held fresh papayas and mangoes. The only concession to the comforts of modern life was a kerosene lamp.

The *kahuna*, a serene-looking man of about seventy, greeted us, and we prepared for the healing and spiritual reading. He had lit incense, and I noticed his vast collection of herbs. Although it was primitive, the place did not evoke a feeling of poverty, but rather a simple, stress-free, energized peacefulness.

I distinctly felt something mystical and free about the man as he began his ritual of preparing to tune into his divine guidance. Guided by spirit energy—he told me that he always felt the presence of his grandparents guiding him from the afterlife—he chanted and hummed as he placed his hands on me and invoked healing energy. I could feel the warm energy radiate from his soul through his gentle hands.

This gifted, empowered *kahuna* could tap into the energy of all of nature, both in the world we could see and in worlds we could not. Since he relied solely on his psychic and spiritual abilities, they had become more developed, he told me. He relied on telepathy instead of a telephone, and on his daily interaction with nature instead of modern conveniences. As he remained open to guidance and messages from animals, the plant world, water, earth, sky, and unseen dimensions, those exchanges were as normal to him as conversations with friends are to us. He trusted the wisdom of the spirits of nature and of his ancestors, and they served him well.

There is a bit of the shaman in all of us—more of it, if we want to open to its development. Physicist Fred Alan Wolf notes in his book *The Eagle's Quest: A Physicist's Search for Truth in the Heart of the Shamanic World* that in living with and studying with shamans all over the world he began to discover his own innate powers.

"How does one become aware of one's own shamanic power?" he writes. "I was seeing a way, although it wasn't as I had expected it. The key is to recognize in one's own experiences the presence of shamanic incidents. These events are always powerful, but when they occur we often tend to dismiss them as foolish, frightening or coincidental without any further merit. These experiences can be thought of as bleed-throughs from a world that is beyond our immediate sense of the common world we all live in."

Communicating with the afterlife is an ability among many that shamans have mastered, an ability that each and every one of us has naturally, and, if we allow it, can grow to its fullest potential.

"The shamans had been teaching me a way to shift my perception so that I became aware of other realities," Wolf explains. Among those realities was the higher dimension that includes the afterlife. Applying the principles of physics to understand more fully the mystical experiences of the shaman (and vice versa), he explains that "from a new physics pinnacle, everything is connected. Life flows between points and doesn't simply begin and end with birth and death."

Science is catching up to the most ancient of mystical beliefs.

Afterlife beliefs may be explained by different rituals, symbols, and stories, but cultures around the globe, from the most ancient times to the modern, all agree on one thing: after we die we all go *someplace*.

We in the modern Western world are tempted to be vague about it all. Some people believe that we go either to heaven or to hell, with all of their archetypal images of angels and devils, bliss and torture, while others declare that the only place we go after death is into the ground, where we become a worm's lunch. There is, however, a rich tradition, very much alive (you'll pardon the pun) today, with its roots in every native culture, that is not based upon fear of death or the reward or punishment of our deeds in the afterlife. This tradition holds that *life* is *life*; we simply live it in different dimensions at different stages of our spiritual development. When we're done here in the three-dimensional earth plane, we pass over to the higher dimensions, where we continue with our life lessons and experiences, but without the physical body we once inhabited.

Where were we before we experienced our earthly life? Also in the dimension that we go to after we "die." The prelife and the afterlife can be thought of as our soul's home base.

"The ancients knew what modern man is just beginning to understand," Joel L. Whitton, M.D., and Joe Fisher remind us in *Life Between Life,* "that the life between life is our natural home from which we venture forth on arduous journeys of physical embodiment."

Teachings of native peoples survive, forming the foundation for modern inquiry in philosophy and science.

Native peoples "were not bothered by the fear of death," Ernest Becker noted in his Pulitzer Prize–winning work, *The Denial of Death.* "Death was, more often than not, accompanied by rejoicing and festivities; that death seemed to be an occasion for celebration rather than fear—because they believe that death is the ultimate promotion, the final ritual elevation to a higher form of life, to the enjoyment of eternity in some form. Most modern Westerners have trouble believing this anymore, which is what makes the fear of death so prominent a part of our psychological make-up."

Perhaps the worst by-product of the last few centuries of Western "progress" is fear. It has become the basis of everything we do and think. Out of fear comes the compulsion to control everything—from nature to one another—rather than to cooperate in harmony with our universe and all who inhabit it. I know that this notion will not come as news to you; both ancient and modern native peoples have been telling it to us forever.

We've seen how centuries of fear-based thinking has brought us nothing more than pain—environmental pain for earth, personal pain for all her peoples. Perhaps we are now more willing to embrace love and harmony with nature and one another as the only healthy, fulfilling way in which to live.

The belief that those who have passed on are lost to us is one of the fears we can most easily banish. Communication with the afterlife has nothing to do with ghosts, evil, or anything negative. It is a perfectly healthy, natural part of life. It should be approached positively, with love and respect.

The Native Americans "saw the whole of life as consisting of the dual quest for wisdom and for divinity," says Alfonso Ortiz, a Tewa Indian, in Dennis and Barbara Tedlock's work *Teachings from the American Earth.* He added that the Native American way is to have a comprehensive double view of the world, while nonnative peoples and other Westerners have lost sight of one whole dimension. The authors noted that Native Americans are individualists and empiricists, meaning that they believe only what they themselves have experienced. The meaning of their spirituality is discovered by reflection, the Tedlocks remind us, not through historical exactness. This is quite the opposite of how we so-called modernists operate, denying the validity of our experiences in a futile quest for outside, objective "proof."

The various Native American tribes have different ways of describing similar phenomena and their spirituality. The Oglala, a Teton Sioux tribe, call the human spirit *sicun,* and believe that each person is blessed with *sicun* at birth to guide and guard them. At death, *sicun* guides the person to the afterlife. This kind of spirit is, then, part of a universal spirit consciousness.

The Zuñi people believe that when someone dies in his sleep, he hasn't really died, per se, but has simply awakened in the afterlife. They also believe that if you die in any other manner, your *pinanne,* the wind of your breath and heart, doesn't proceed directly to the afterlife, but instead stays around your home for four days. If the spirit has difficulty with the idea of leaving, it may visit loved ones in their dreams. After four days, the *pinanne* walks off to the afterlife.

The Zuñi call humans *Tek'ohannan aaho"i*, which means "People of the Light," because the Sun Father brought them from darkness to live in his light.

Death is called "the end of the light," and the more lessons a person has learned in life on earth, the better that person will fare in the afterlife, which the Zuñi consider the real, original world.

The concept of living in the light, with the earthly plane being merely a place to learn lessons before returning "home," is fundamental to most native cultures and the majority of civilizations in recorded history.

In ancient Greece, God spoke to people through enlightened, spiritually attuned people called *oracles*. Today, spiritual communication often comes through modern-day shamans, mediums, intuitives, and everyday folks who remain open to spiritual communication.

Seth is an entity who was channeled through Jane Roberts. Roberts wrote a series of acclaimed books containing the teachings of this spiritual being, who defines the soul as "an electromagnetic energy field" and "nonphysical consciousness," descriptions that are common among mystics and scientists alike. None other than Thomas Edison even worked at scientific experiments on the soul, trying up until his death to invent an electrical instrument that would enable him to communicate with the afterlife. Today, scientists at major universities study the electromagnetic energy of *chi*, what the Chinese call the life force or soul.

The use of fire is present in many cultural rites and

mythology surrounding the spirit. Buddhists in Nepal write the name of the deceased on a piece of paper, then burn the paper to assist the soul's release out of the body and into the transition from the earthly plane to the afterlife. The Balinese practice cremation to release the departed's soul for reincarnation. The legendary bird the phoenix, a symbol of immortality, bursts into flame, then rises from the ashes as a renewed being, both physically and in spirit. The image of the bird as a metaphor for the soul is common among many native peoples and cultures, signifying the soul's ability to fly. Early Egyptians used the bird as a symbol for the soul. The *ba,* a bird with a human head, flew around in the afterlife, according to ancient Egyptian teachings.

The ancient Romans believed that birds, particularly eagles, guided human souls to a paradise afterlife. The afterlife, they believe, existed parallel to the world of the living on earth. This belief was common to native peoples and early civilizations everywhere, as far back as the Neanderthals, who took the concept of a parallel afterlife quite literally, assuming that physical needs there would be similar to those on the earthly plane. When they buried their dead, they also buried food and other practical items with them, so they could take them to the afterlife.

The Egyptians also believed that those who had passed on would need earthly possessions in the afterlife and placed them in pyramids with the carefully mummified bodies of the dead, following rituals prescribed in *The Egyptian Book of the Dead* (its title translates from the ancient language as *The Coming Forth from Day*) so that the soul would be properly guided into the afterlife. The ritual began with the words, "You have not gone away dead, you have gone away alive."

If we are never actually dead, then why do we not consciously remember our existence as souls leading "lives" in the prelife/afterlife higher dimension?

Eastern philosophy holds that it is actually a blessing that we don't automatically remember. Mohandas K. "Mahatma" Gandhi once said that "it is nature's kindness that we do not remember past births. Life would be a burden if we carried such a tremendous load of memories."

To remember past lives on the three-dimensional earth plane in the universe and elsewhere, *and* in the higher-dimensional prelife/afterlife realm—it would indeed be overwhelming to carry those memories with us on a conscious level! We do, of course, have access to all of what we are and all of what we have learned, for it all lies within the many layers of our human consciousness, within our soul.

There are Eastern philosophies that tell us that each soul, before entering the three-dimensional earth plane in a body, passes through an etheric, or dimensional, barrier that lowers the vibrations of its consciousness, thereby blocking automatic conscious memory of its existence in the glorious higher dimensions. Why? To keep us from the pain of missing our true home, and to enable us to focus on the continuation of our soul's journey in learning its lessons as it proceeds toward total enlightenment without the distraction of homesickness or conscious remembrance of past life karma.

This barrier has been called the River of Forgetfulness. As our consciousness increases, so does our ability to remember. All mystical traditions teach that all of our experiences are simply reminders of what, deep inside, we *already* know, hence the often used term "awakening" to describe our various stages of enlightenment. It's as if we have been spiritually asleep, and as we mature we wake up, step by step. Even in our earthly bodies we can attain a great deal of connectedness with the universe in all its dimensions and with the spiritual energy of all that is within it. The Native Americans call this energy All Our Relations; it includes not only everyone and everything that exists on earth (animate and inanimate) right now, but also everything from the past and in the future, as well as absolutely everything else in the cosmos. "Everything, both known and unknown is included in this phrase of wholeness and holiness," notes Brooke Medicine Eagle, psychologist, Native American spiritual leader, and author of *Buffalo Woman Comes Singing*. "Holiness is never understood to be focusing attention on a white-bearded old man figure as God, or on any specific spiritual figure, but rather enlarging our awareness to consciously include and respectfully consider All That Is, All Our Relations—all beings, energies, and things in the larger Circle of Life."

What the spiritual life of native peoples the world over and those following Eastern thought have in common—and what is also the basis of today's reawakened spirituality—is the power of individual knowingness and experience as the true guidance. Brooke Medicine Eagle puts it quite bluntly, and correctly, when she says, "Connecting with the Great Spirit within is a profound and absolutely vital task if you are to pursue a spiritual path. To begin the quest by thinking that someone else has the connection—that power lies outside of you—means that you are not even on the path."

Teachings about death and the afterlife are presented in symbol and ritual; through all manner of creative expression including music, drama, art, architecture, dance, theater; through nature, healing, and the spoken and written word. *The Egyptian Book of the Dead* is but one example.

The Tibetan Book of the Dead similarly assists the dying through the process of leaving their physical body, and tells them what to expect in the various stages of the soul's after-death journey. More accurately, it describes the *interlife,* forty-nine days in which the soul, now without a body, prepares for its next incarnation, according to Buddhist beliefs. The interlife is called the *bardo,* thus the book's Tibetan title, *Bardo Thodol,* meaning "Liberation by Hearing on the After-Death Plane."

Both books, said the late Oxford scholar W. Y. Evans-Wentz, who edited the English translation and coined the name of *The Tibetan Book of the Dead,* teach "an Art of Dying and Coming Forth into a New life." Dr. Carl Jung, writing a psychological commentary to *The Tibetan Book of the Dead* (in a Swiss edition in 1938, then published in an English translation in 1955), noted that the book "caused a considerable stir in English-speaking countries at the time of its first appearance in 1927." The average Westerner believes, Jung wrote, that "the soul is something pitifully small, unworthy, personal, subjective and a lot more besides. He therefore prefers to use the word 'mind' instead." Yet, as Jung points out, "it is the soul, which by the divine creative power inherent in it, makes the metaphysical assertion; it posits the distinctions between metaphysical entities. Not only is it the condition of all metaphysical reality, it *is* that reality."

Jung concludes that "it is highly sensible of the *Bardo Thodol* to make clear to the dead man the primacy of the soul, for that is the one thing which life does not make clear to us . . . this is a truth which in the face of all evidence, in the greatest things as in the smallest, is never known, although it is often so very necessary, indeed vital, for us to know it."

Within most Western religious institutions, Jung reports, regrettably little attention is paid to the soul's journey. "The Catholic Church is the only place in the world of the white man where any provision is made for the souls of the departed. Inside the Protestant camp, with its world-affirming optimism, we only find a few mediumistic 'rescue circles,' whose main concern is to make the dead aware of the fact that they *are* dead. . . . Apart from the Masses said for the soul in the Catholic Church, the provisions we make for the dead are rudimentary and on the lowest level, not because we cannot convince ourselves of the soul's immortality, but because we have rationalized [that] psychological need out of existence. We behave as if we did not have this need, and because we cannot believe in a life after death we prefer to do nothing about it."

In his foreword to an Oxford University Press translation of *The Tibetan Book of the Dead,* Lama Anagarika Govinda humorously remarks: "It may be argued that nobody can talk about death with authority who has not died; and since nobody, apparently, has ever returned from death, how can anybody knows what death is, or what happens after it? The Tibetan will answer: 'There is not *one* person, indeed, not *one* living being, that has *not* returned from death. In fact, we all have died many deaths, before we came into this incarnation. And what we call birth is merely the reverse side of death, like one of the two sides of a coin, or like a door which we call 'entrance' from outside and 'exit' from inside a room."

As the modern literature on the subject reveals, scores of people around the world have also come back from Near Death Experiences to their current lives with startling reports of the interlife and afterlife.

The Old Testament, when introducing Adam and Eve, affirms our inherent spiritual nature by stating, "Ye shall not surely die" but "shall be as gods" (Genesis 3:4,5), implying that life, in one form or another, is eternal.

The New Testament, with its emphasis on belief in Jesus Christ as Savior and redemption from sin as the ticket into an eternal afterlife, states: "If ye live after the flesh, ye shall die: but if ye through the Spirit do mortify the deeds of the body, ye shall live" (Romans 8:13).

Man's immortality "was conditioned on sinlessness, holiness, a retention of the image of God in which he was created," when man was initially created, explains C. B. Haynes, in his book *When a Man Dies*. "If man is to obtain immortality, he must obtain it in and through Christ, its source." The Christian view of the afterlife is plainly stated in Romans 6:23—"The gift of God is eternal life through Jesus Christ our Lord," and on the conditions set forth in Romans 2:7, that immortality is granted "to them who by patient continuance in well doing seek for glory and honor and immortality."

The bottom line in Christianity is, then, "He that

soweth to the Spirit shall of the Spirit reap life everlasting" (Galatians 6:8).

The nondenominational view of death and the afterlife holds that we are each on a spiritual journey, and that after death our souls, or spirits, move into another dimension. There are some physicists who believe it to be the fifth dimension, an expansion into a higher spatial dimension beyond the three dimensions our five senses can perceive within "normal" consciousness. Within this higher dimension we continue to have experiences, learn life lessons and teach them, as well as having the ability to reach back over to the three-dimensional plane to offer guidance and interact with those still "living" on the earthly plane. Our life lessons may also continue through reincarnation.

Greek philosophers, as well as those of the East, taught the principles of reincarnation. Pythagoras introduced the concept to Greek culture, theorizing that after death the soul would ultimately be reborn into a new body, human or animal. Other Greek philosophers spoke of what we now call Out of Body Experiences (OBEs). They believed that a soul could leave the body during life for out-of-body travels. In fact, the word *ecstasy*, to the Greeks, was translated to mean "out of the body." They also taught that the soul was connected to the divine. The Greek philosophies of the soul are considered now to be the beginning of the modern idea of the immortal soul.

Socrates believed that death was the release of the soul from "the chains of the body." Plato was the first Western philosopher to discuss the concept of soul and body. He believed that the soul, in fact, exists before the body is created, as well as after it dies, and that the soul, not the body, is the *real* person.

Early Christianity taught that reincarnation provided the soul with many experiences in many lives to work toward the enlightenment and purification needed to take up residence in heaven. In a political move, the teaching of reincarnation was removed from Christian doctrine in 553 at the Second Council of Constantinople.

In his great work *De Anima* (Of the Soul), Aristotle taught that the soul animates the body, makes it alive, and that all living creatures and plants have souls. He placed the human soul, however, as the most evolved. Although he learned the concept of the eternal soul from Plato, by his later years Aristotle abandoned the notion of human beings' having an immortal soul, saying that only God's soul could enjoy that distinction. Those philosophers who believed that there was an interconnectedness between the Creator and man would argue that by divine connection man's soul would also be eternal.

Seventeenth-century philosopher René Descartes ("I think, therefore I am") believed that reality was composed of the mental and the physical. The mental/spiritual reality, he asserted, is manifested by thinking; the physical is what can be measured by its extension into space. He did not address the effects the mind and body had on each other, however. He believed that the soul lives in the body only until the body dies, and that nothing can destroy the soul. He theorized that the pineal gland, located in the back of the head, was the physical home of the soul when it resided in the body.

The Age of Enlightenment placed the emphasis of man's search for knowledge in the realm of reason and science, not religion, where it had previously resided. Within this movement came the notion that the truth could be found only in one's own perceptions and experiences—the philosophy of *empiricism.*

The validity of empirical knowledge—I felt it, I sensed it, I experienced it, therefore it is true for me—persists to this day, playing a role not only in spirituality but in science as well.

In 1781, philosopher Immanuel Kant published *The Critique of Pure Reason,* stating that although knowledge comes from what we perceive, our minds interpret everything that comes in subjectively. Therefore, he concludes, objectivity and any notion of an ultimate reality are not possible; they are beyond knowing. He took no stand on whether the soul is immortal, since according to his philosophy, that question is impossible to answer objectively. He did theorize, though, that humans feel compelled to believe in an immortal soul because we find that notion comforting.

In his landmark work *Nature,* published in 1836, Ralph Waldo Emerson, poet, writer, and philosopher, described the soul as something "through which the universal spirit speaks to the individual, and strives to lead back the individual to it." He also wrote that there is a "correspondence between the human soul and everything that exists in the world," concluding that "the highest revelation is that God is in every man."

Emerson wrote, he said, "to awake in man and to raise the feeling of his worth." What is most important in each person's life? To Emerson, "the one thing in the world, of value, is the active soul."

Leading the mid-nineteenth-century movement of Transcendentalism, Emerson personified its basic tenets: that the mind transcends matter and that we can *know* more than our senses or experiences show us. Among others in this New England–based American philosophical movement were many of the day's most renowned artists, writers, educators, and philosophers, including Henry David Thoreau, author of *Walden*.

The spiritual resurgence of the late twentieth century is very much an extension of what was begun by the Transcendentalists more than one hundred years ago. Transcendentalism was and is today a one-on-one spirituality that rejects the notion of any religious institution or authority, preferring to place the emphasis on each individual's direct experience with the divine, the creative, the inspired, the universal. Its philosophy states that reality lies within the world of the soul, the spirit, and our visible world is actually only a symbol of that true spiritual world.

We all "enjoy an original relation to the universe," Emerson said. That means that we are all part of "that Unity, that over-soul, within which every man's particular being is contained and made one with all others." Man's soul, then, is the soul of the universe.

"Our notions of law and harmony are commonly confined to those instances which we detect," wrote Thoreau in *Walden,* "but the harmony which results from a far greater number of seemingly conflicting, but really concurring laws, which we have not detected, is still more wonderful."

The spiritual world, then, runs often undetected through our physical world—undetected, that is, until we learn to recognize the signs of its presence.

In eighteenth- and nineteenth-century Eastern Europe, Jewish mysticism experienced a reemergence, highlighted by the Hasidic movement, which addressed a basic spirituality that includes belief in an eternal soul and reincarnation, known as *gilgul*.

At the root of Jewish spirituality is the notion that man's "body is earthly, but his soul is heavenly." The afterlife, in mystical Judaism, is alternately referred to as "the world to come," and in a 1984 essay entitled "Life after Death and the World to Come," noted Israeli rabbinical teacher Rabbi Eliyahu Ben Shlomo of the Ohel Yaakov Yeshiva College in B'nei Brak remarked that wondering whether there is life after death "is not the same as wondering if there is life on Mars or conducting experiments in mathematics, chemistry, physics or even biology. The question of life after death is of fundamental importance to our lives *now*. We yearn to know whether our individual existence will last only several score years until we are reduced to non-being by death, or whether we shall continue to exist once our life on earth is over."

Mid-twentieth-century rabbi Yechezkail Levenstein, who taught in Poland, New York, and Jerusalem, made it quite simple when he stated that "the most fundamental concept to work on is to increasingly become aware of the value of the afterlife, and to realize how little this world has to offer in comparison. By internalizing this attitude you will not allow either physical or material bias to rule your actions in life."

Quoting the scholar Rambam, Ben Shlomo reminds us that "as the blind cannot comprehend colors and the deaf comprehend sound, so corporeal men cannot understand the pleasures of the soul . . . and cannot know in this material world what spiritual pleasure means."

Ben Shlomo says that we are limited by our senses because "the things that thrill men's hearts and bring the soul satisfaction and warmth, are precisely those things that are beyond the senses."

What moves us to search for spiritual answers? "The thirst of man's soul cannot be slaked with only a murky token of truth; it seeks the whole truth and will not rest until it has found it," he says, echoing surely the sentiments of those following an individual spiritual path or adhering to the teachings of Judaism, Christianity, Islam, Buddhism, Hinduism, or any native people's spirituality.

In spiritual Judaism, he says, "all the forces of the spirit are activated by our inner self, which is independent of our bodies and senses. . . . Something inside of us determines what is true and what is fraudulent, what is honorable and what is shameful, what is just, honest and ethical and what wicked, iniquitous and base. This 'something' is the soul."

The soul, he continues, "is autonomous. Only its independent existence can explain its willingness to act in opposition to the interests of the body in which it resides. . . . The reality of the soul is one of the most unequivocal certainties of our existence, yet it cannot readily be articulated. Most languages define it as a 'spiritual reality.' A spiritual reality can never die nor cease to be. Death has dominion only over the body."

An afterlife, he says, follows this logic. "The soul, since it is of the spirit and exists independently, is not bound by the laws of matter. Thus, our recognition of the existence of the soul entails the certainty of its continued existence after death—life after death."

Citing the works of philosophers dating back thousands of years, Ben Shlomo says that they have found many forms of logic with which to discuss the soul, and that the soul's existence and immortality are self-evident. "Like all great truths," he states, "it is eminently simple and obvious to any reasonable person."

While science shows us that energy does not die, but merely changes form, spiritual Judaic thought comes to the same conclusion. Quoting the writings of Rambam once again, Ben Shlomo presents the root from which all discussion of the afterlife springs: "Nothing has been lost since the Creation of the world . . . only in the sense that matter returns to its elements—that is, it only changes form but does not cease to exist—and this is the loss of all things lost, for as long as the world exists, this is even more true of the soul which is exalted. It cannot be abolished or lost."

Since "God created man in His own image," as the Old Testament states, it would follow that man's soul is immortal, since the Creator's obviously is, conclude centuries of Jewish philosophers.

The afterlife, or "the world to come," is called *olam haba,* meaning "world of souls." Jewish spiritual philosophy is much like Eastern philosophy in the belief that what we do in this life, the time in which the soul resides in this body, determines what will happen to the soul in the afterlife and, indeed, forever. "This is the whole purpose of our life in this world," writes Ben Shlomo. Once again, the belief that our earthly life (or lives) is a series of lessons and experiences that continue in the afterlife, and the better we do here, the higher a spiritual level we will attain in the afterlife. "Take you therefore very good care of your souls," goes the saying from the Torah.

As in Eastern philosophy and also the spiritual teachings of most native peoples, Jewish mysticism holds that in the afterlife "neither the reward nor the punishment that awaits us is physical," Ben Shlomo explains, adding that "the reward in the next world is not remuneration received in return for his actions (in the earthly plane), but rather the individual himself prepares and creates his own 'world to come.'"

As old and new thought both reveal, the afterlife is what you make it.

Central to both Hinduism and Buddhism is our karmic fate: what we will experience in our afterlife and next lives is determined by our behavior in our present life. Just how long do these life cycles continue? Reincarnation theory states that we don't stop reincarnating until we have achieved complete enlightenment and total union with the Universe (the Creator, the Higher Power, God, or whatever term you're most comfortable with).

The soul's immortality is celebrated in Japan during the annual Bon Festival, when it is believed that the spirits of those who have passed on visit the living to offer inspiration, guidance, and wisdom. To help the spirits symbolically find their loved ones, candles are lit on paths in cemeteries so the souls can find their way back to their places of burial.

In Indonesia death is celebrated, not mourned, since it is believed that the soul is being freed from the earthly prison of the body. That same attitude of reverence and celebration is found in Bali, where the occasion is marked not by burial but by cremation, as a symbolic separation of the soul from the body and a purifying of the spirit so that it may move on to its next life.

In Nigeria, the Ijaw tribe builds houses over the graves of loved ones, to symbolize their belief that the dead are in some way still dwelling among the living.

Although we are perhaps the most skeptical nation on the planet, Americans' fascination with what happens to us after death has resulted in the subject's being studied scientifically, sociologically, and psychologically as well as spiritually by researchers across the country.

In one of the largest studies of its kind, for example, Sukie Miller, a U.S. psychotherapist, is leading the Death and Dying II Project, gathering, studying, and cataloging information from cultures the world over, amassing beliefs, rituals, myths, writings, oral traditions, art forms, and the like about what lies after physical death. The project's research and study results will be shared with educators, the clergy, health care and hospice professionals, therapists, students, and the general public, who are as spiritually curious as ever.

We have always known that the physical world is not all there is to existence. In all our attempts to understand the world that lies beyond our senses, we have created philosophies, religions, myths, legends, artistic expression, and scientific study, as well as the unfortunate by-products fear, prejudice, war, greed, and an unnatural reliance on manipulative external power. We have often focused our attention anywhere and everywhere but where we *should* be looking: within ourselves. Our answers come from our experiences, our flashes of insight, our intuitive universal guidance, our natural connectedness with everything and everyone that defies all barriers, even the perceived barrier of physical death.

CHAPTER TWO

Just Visiting

Imagine having the ability to travel to the fifth dimension—home of the spiritual realms, the afterlife, and prelife—and then come right back to this body and this life. It happens every day to people all over the world. It's not an ability reserved just for shamans, mystics, and the spiritual adepts. As we open our hearts and minds to the range of our consciousness possibilities we can see that we already possess these abilities and often use them without realizing that we are doing so.

When we dream, our minds travel while our physical bodies remain behind. Though we may have the appearance of a physical body with us in a dream, we also have unlimited travel possibilities. We can go anywhere, do anything, see anyone. Some of us have learned how to program our dreams so that we can order up exactly what we want, like choosing from a restaurant's menu, instead of being limited to whatever we happen to be served.

The Out of Body Experience (OBE) operates in a similar manner, yet it is *distinctly* different. In a dream we do not have the same conscious awareness that we have when we're fully awake. In an OBE we do.

Research into the OBE has shown us that consciousness can separate from physical reality. During the OBE state, the mind is awake while the body is asleep, revealing that "human mind-consciousness can operate, think, reason, feel without the strong physical sensory input signals previously deemed necessary," according to the country's premier OBE researcher, Robert A. Monroe. Monroe is the founder of the Monroe Institute and author of three books on the subject, including the recently published *Ultimate Journey*. "The key implication is that one is indeed 'more' than the physical body, that one can exist without it."

This state is the equivalent of the delta state, a state of brain activity that occurs when the body is in a deep sleep. During OBE, the mind is completely awake and in full control.

Much of what we are learning now about the higher-dimensional realm and the afterlife is coming from the experiences of the thousands and thousands whose OBEs are being studied as well as the many who report Near Death Experiences (NDEs).

The Monroe Institute, for example, has documented

and studied the OBEs of people (including Monroe himself) that include "trips" to the afterlife dimension. While there, they speak and interact with those who have passed on, and they are free to travel to a number of places. One of these sites, which Monroe calls The Park, is essentially a welcoming center for new arrivals who are no longer alive in their physical bodies in the earth plane—what we used to call "the dead." At The Park, amid lush surroundings that include nearly every conceivable variety of flora and fauna, spiritual beings appear in human form to help ease the person in the emotional transition from the physical world to the afterlife plane. Apparently, some have difficulty accepting that they are now dead and residents of the afterlife. Monroe, during an OBE, visited another such place created to help spirits in transition, which he found while looking for a friend who had passed on. It looks exactly like a doctor's office, and is one that doctors can go to after they've been counseled and processed at The Park. He was told that recently passed on "medical types, physicians, surgeons and so on" come there "to calm down after the big change. They need it because they have been so locked into keeping patients alive. But they recover quickly in a familiar environment."

Spiritual beings, some of whom have previously "lived" on earth's three-dimensional plane, are assigned to places like this doctor's office suite to assist souls in adjusting to the afterlife.

A very dear friend of mine, Bob, who passed away from complications of AIDS, has told me from the afterlife that he is now part of a group of people who help those who die of AIDS-related illnesses in their transition. Before passing on, Bob worked in the medical field, so he is especially valuable to this group in the afterlife.

In this spiritual dimension, thought can create anything, so whatever is needed to assist anyone of any profession, background, or culture through the transition is immediately available.

People who have had OBEs report that the afterlife is, indeed, a *culture*. They see the society, the buildings, and the landscape that human thought has created over there. They watch people at work, at leisure, and studying.

Those who have NDEs come back with a different kind of information about the afterlife. They travel the same route that the dead do (they are actually dead at the time, even though they are later revived) and so they often report passing through a tunnel, and being drawn into a light, being compelled by a great power over which they have no control. This is unlike an OBE experience, in which travel is voluntary. During an NDE, the person often is met by loved ones who have passed on (they're the ones who ultimately tell the person that he or she cannot remain in the afterlife and must return to the body). Some people who are clinically dead for a long period get so far into the afterlife that they experience a Life Review, in which they are shown what looks like a complete and almost instantaneous panoramic movie of their lives. While viewing this "movie" they not only reexperience everything they've ever done, thought, or felt, but feel the impact of all their good and bad deeds and actions from the point of view of everyone in their lives. This way they can feel the emotions, for example, of everyone they ever made happy or hurt.

Many NDEs include a journey through a most spec-
tacular aspect of the afterlife, one filled with magical, ethereal images of color and sound, breathtakingly gorgeous
scenery unlike anything in nature as we know it on earth:
massive crystalline cities, skies and bodies of water in vivid
colors other than the usual range of blues, and floating
beings of light. They also report the ability to communicate
telepathically, to understand information simply from hearing musical tones and seeing light and color displays that
far surpass any laser show or fireworks display we could
imagine.

Raymond A. Moody, Jr., M.D., a pioneer in the study
of NDEs, reports that those who experience these phenomena liken the emotional feeling to a homecoming. Despite
the markedly different surroundings they may find themselves in or their strong feelings for those they've left
behind, they are met in the afterlife with a feeling of intense
love, peace, well-being, and belonging. The author of many
books on NDEs, including the classic *Life After Life,* Moody
now also runs a research center where he studies afterlife
communication, focusing on the ability to literally see the
image of someone who has passed on.

In one of the most astounding accounts of a journey
to the afterlife and back as an NDE, Dannion Brinkley
described being taught by spiritual beings and being shown
117 prophetic visions, 95 of which have come true since he
had the experience twenty years ago. In his recent book,
Saved by the Light, Brinkley also discusses his mission, given
to him by thirteen beings of light: to build stress-reduction

and healing centers around the country that would incorporate holistic practices as well as sophisticated equipment, heretofore unknown to modern science, intricately described to Brinkley by these spiritual beings.

After his first NDE, which occurred in 1975 when he was hit by lightning, he continued to be taught by these spiritual beings for many years in vivid dreams and deeper levels of consciousness. Brinkley experienced a second NDE a few years ago while undergoing heart surgery, during which other spiritual beings instructed him further. Amid calming sounds, colors, and scents he was told, "This is the feeling you are supposed to create in the centers."

Brinkley's work creating these healing centers continues and he has already designed a special bed that facilitates the deep level of consciousness achieved when having an Out of Body Experience. It is in use at Raymond Moody's research center in rural Alabama.

Brinkley and others who have had NDEs also report that while in the afterlife they have the ability to see energy fields, and use their five senses in heightened and overlapping ways: feeling color, for example.

In dreams, we also gain some insight into the higher-dimensional realms and the afterlife. My mother would often visit with her late parents in dreams. There my grandmother would cook, my grandfather would tend his garden, and both would talk about her life with her, answering her questions and giving valuable advice. The settings in such dreams vary, as we'll see in the experience stories that follow in Part Two. They can take place in what appear to be ordinary three-dimensional earth plane locations, both indoors and outdoors, or they can have an ethereal, otherworldly quality that may indeed imply a visit to the afterlife dimension. Before my mother passed away, she had contacts with the afterlife in her dreams from her childhood right through adulthood. In one dream, she went fishing with her late brother. After my father passed away he would often visit my mother in dreams, and in one she was in a half-awake, half-asleep state in which she could feel the weight of his body sitting on her bed. His energy was clearly present and filtering through to this dimension.

Dr. Michael Persinger, a researcher at Laurentian University in Canada, has concluded that there is actually a change in the level of human energy during what are considered transcendental experiences. He has found that bursts of unusually high levels of electricity in the brain are present when a so-called psychic event occurs, suggesting an enhanced brain less constrained by time or space.

We humans, even in our physical form, are beings of energy who vibrate at different levels, who have the capacity to increase our vibratory frequency and to be more sensitive to the energy frequencies of other dimensions as well.

George Anderson, perhaps one of the most often studied and tested expert intuitives, is gifted with the ability to consistently receive afterlife communication. He is the subject of the bestseller *We Don't Die: George Anderson's Conversations with the Other Side,* in which he explains that "we feel a sense of being uplifted in the next stage of life. When we become one in the next dimension, we feel that we understand everything, we feel spiritually and emotionally up-lifted. That's probably where the conception of going up came from."

When asked if everyone in the afterlife is automati-cally living in bliss, George replied, "I've never really heard any complaints about the other side, unless the person has gone over there and into the darker levels, for committing some serious crime, hurting people, or committing suicide. Generally, though, most spirits I've heard from seem to be very happy, very content, very much at peace, very aware and knowing of themselves, even if they were very negative and very unhappy here."

Where does this peace come from?

"Learning and growing seem to be what it's all about there," he says. "And they are able to understand them-selves, *if* they want to. I've been told by the other side that you have to make a prime decision over there. You have to face up to yourself and do something about it, otherwise you'll just flounder and you won't progress spiritually."

Part of this growth, according to all who have had contact with the afterlife, is the lessons you learn not only from spiritual beings, but from *service*.

"It's like having a job here," George says. "You just take on a spiritual job in the next stage of life, where you earn your soul progression by helping others crossing over, by helping people here find their way spiritually, helping peo-ple there to find their way spiritually, to be involved in var-ious sorts of things."

Through free will, each soul, no matter how much in darkness it is when it arrives in the afterlife, can progress to the light. It also does not matter which religious traditions you may follow while on the earthly plane. Once in the afterlife, there are no denominations. As George Anderson has been told repeatedly by those who have passed over, "The one way is within yourself."

PART TWO

Continued Life,

❋

Continued

Communication

*What happens after death is so unspeakably glorious
that our imagination and our feelings do not suffice to
form even an approximate conception of it.*

CARL JUNG, *Letters, vol. I*

CHAPTER THREE

Life on the Other Side

In the late twentieth century we see that
as human evolution progresses with a
profound shift to a higher consciousness,
fear is giving way to knowledge and understanding. What we called a ghost in
the nineteenth century, we now call a
spiritual energy. We no longer react to the
unknown with a negative attitude, but
instead acknowledge our thirst for knowledge and our innate love of possibilities,
mystery, heightened awareness, and nature.

We are learning to honor our experiences, follow our inner guidance, and
seek to transcend barriers. We honor the
infinite realities of nature, the evolution
of our consciousness, the shifts and

expansion of our perceptions, and our true birthrights that we have, unfortunately, at times let fear inhibit and dull.

We go into deeper, relaxed states for healing, divination, contact with higher dimensions, communication with the afterlife and spiritual beings, and our quest for the meaning of life in general and our individual purpose.

We know that we are pure energy beings who happen for a time to inhabit physical bodies. One day we will shed those bodies like a butterfly emerging from a cocoon.

The higher dimension we seek to understand and communicate with is—as perceived by an unenlightened, unawakened consciousness from the three-dimensional earth plane—an unseen world. It is the world from which we came, and to which we all return when our bodies physically die.

So, we want to know: *What's going on over there?*

AFTER DEATH

After physical death, the spirit evolves toward spiritual perfection in a world of inconceivable beauty and pleasure. Most of us are greeted by friends and loved ones, familiar spirits, guardian spirits, or master souls. We can see and hear, feel, smell, and taste. Our five senses are heightened and expanded to include the ability to communicate telepathically and to *sense* things that on the three-dimensional earth plane we could experience only in ways that were limited by our inhabiting a physical body.

As a spirit moves toward the realm of light, it sloughs off the emotional attachments to its earthly existence. Those spirits who are not informed about the afterlife prior to their deaths may find everything rather puzzling. They will be aware that they have a body of sorts, a shining, luminous body, and they discover that they can pass through objects without hindrance. Travel is a simple matter of wishing to be somewhere. Anything can be created instantaneously simply by thinking it.

The spirit encounters spiritual beings who present to it a mirror of what the spirit experienced in its earthly life—all its actions, thoughts and deeds. This Life Review enables the spirit to actually judge *itself*.

Beautiful, majestic music fills this higher dimension, sounds known on earth as "music of the spheres." The spirit feels ecstasy, peace, love, bliss, joy, glory, relief, acceptance, and instant knowingness of a Higher Creative Power and Life's Purpose. Dark, negative, or less highly evolved souls are much less aware of these positive feelings, and one of their initial tasks in the afterlife is to work toward shedding their negativity. These souls occupy lower energy levels in the afterlife, but definitely *not* what we have been led to believe about "hell." The lower levels of the afterlife can be likened to lower grades in school. Some souls enter the afterlife at a first-grade level, for example, while others may enter at fifth or ninth grade, or go straight to college or graduate school. Within each level certain lessons are learned, duties performed, and communication access to the earthly plane made possible in varying degrees, depending upon your spiritual growth and awareness.

LEVELS

In the afterlife you live on a spiritual level with those of a like mind, a like consciousness, and like vibrations. Your goal is to evolve to a higher level of consciousness. Those on lower levels, such as those who have committed serious crimes, aren't allowed to communicate with us on the earthly plane until they've progressed to a higher level. However, other spirit beings can pass communications from them to us.

These levels are vibratory levels. We evolve and grow higher and higher in vibration until we become one with God, the Higher Power, the Creative Force, the Great Spirit. Every spirit in the afterlife has a chance for hope and evolution. Free will operates there just as it does here on the three-dimensional earthly plane.

Not everyone is having a wonderful time frolicking in the afterlife. People are exactly where they were spiritually when they died, and their Life Review begins the process of clearing and resolving their past, their individual issues. A spirit with the desire to progress is helped to evolve by the many spiritual guides inhabiting the afterlife. Without that desire, a spirit cannot progress. Those with addictions, for example, can strive to break free from them, or use their ability to create matter from thought to manifest endless supplies of whatever they were addicted to on the earthly plane, thus plunging themselves even further into pain, darkness, and the negative cycle of addiction.

When you are a spirit, you can visit with others on your level or one of the levels below you, but you *cannot* visit a higher level. You can only ascend when you have *evolved* up by learning and living spiritual lessons of love, compassion, respect, and connectedness. Only under very special circumstances, and when accompanied by a spiritual guide, can a human spirit visit a level above where it currently exists.

DAILY LIFE

Spirits can create *anything* in the afterlife that they want: any environment, any object, and food, drink, or substance, just by thinking of it. Travel is also propelled by thought. Simply think and you can be fishing, enjoying an amusement park, sitting on top of a majestic mountain, or conducting a symphony. Spirits can create a setting that reminds them of the earthly plane or create surroundings of color, light, sound, and energy unique to the higher dimension in their ethereal beauty, form, and function.

As a spirit, you also have lessons to learn, schools and classes to go to, job responsibilities, organizations to work with, guidelines and duties of all kinds depending upon your spiritual vibratory level, your talents, interests, personal issues, and often, your previous situation on the earthly plane.

Once you've settled in, you may, for example, work for a while counseling and guiding new arrivals with whom you have something in common, or you may be part of a soul group that guides those still living in bodies on the earthly plane. These soul groups offer guidance in every area imaginable—professional, artistic, medical, political, sociological, and personal. Spirits in this higher dimension monitor the earthly plane very closely in order to give us as much spiritual assistance as possible. They work with us in great joy and love, helping us to increase our vibrations. The higher your vibration—the more you live in light, peace, harmony, compassion, and love—the more advanced a soul you are when you return "home" to the higher-dimensional realm of the afterlife. Love, harmony, and realization of the oneness, the interconnectedness of the energy of human beings to one another and everything else in the universe, is a connection that transcends *all* dimensions. It is what enables our vibrations to increase while we're on the earthly plane and even further when we enter the higher-dimensional realm that is also home to the afterlife.

When living in the afterlife you are not only with those you knew from the earthly plane, but you meet new human spirits and other spiritual beings who are more advanced, many of whom have not lived in a human body. At first, when you are entering the afterlife, the spirits of those you knew in your earthly life and special guardian beings come to you primarily to ease the loneliness of the transition from physical death to the spiritual dimension. Other beings of brilliant light appear then, too, with unconditional enveloping love. All of the spirits in the afterlife—those you knew before and those you are just meeting—remain available to you.

In the afterlife you communicate by speaking and by telepathy or thought transference.

Love is the highest vibrational frequency, and fear is the lowest in this realm, just as on the three-dimensional earthly plane.

CHILDREN

Children who enter the afterlife spend as much time as they need close to their loved ones who are also in the afterlife. As on the earthly plane, they spend time at play as well as on learning. Children often initially adjust much more easily to this higher dimension than adults because their minds are clearer, cleaner, purer, and more spiritual. The light enters into these young spirits very quickly because they are so open.

ENERGY VIBRATION

When we are still in our human bodies, we can quicken the vibrational frequency of our energy. You have probably felt this before, but perhaps haven't labeled it as a vibrational frequency shift. Think about how you feel when you are in the connected, peaceful (yet energized!), joyous state of mind often induced by music; being on or near the water, in the mountains, the forest, or some other natural setting. Think about how you feel when you pray or meditate, dance or do yoga exercises. Think about the experience of being with someone you love. This is the oneness with the universe, with a Higher Power, with Love, with Nature, that the mystics and philosophers have always spoken of and experienced. This oneness is a feeling that *everyone* can have. This feeling of connectedness raises our vibrations.

Key to increasing vibration on the earthly plane is a healthy, toxin-free physical body, fed by plenty of natural, organic foods that provide nutrients that stimulate the body's energy and the brain's electrical circuits.

In the higher-dimensional realms, the body no longer affects the spirit's vibration, because it has been left behind, either temporarily or permanently. The spirit's vibration increases further and further in the higher-dimensional realm, the afterlife, the ultimate being a vibration of pure light, thus the term "enlightenment."

INTERDIMENSIONAL TRAVEL

We can interact with someone who's now "living" in the afterlife, in a dream, a vision, a meditative state, during an OBE, NDE, or any other kind of vibrational state when our consciousness is expanded. Does this experience take place on the three-dimensional earthly plane or in the higher-dimensional realm in which the afterlife exists?

The short answer is: it all depends on the situation.

Our soul does travel to the fifth dimension when we're having an OBE or an NDE, and quite often when we are in one of the other expanded states of consciousness, too.

While science has yet to figure out how to get our *bodies* to the higher-dimensional realm, our *souls* have always been able to make the trip there both as temporary visitors and permanent residents.

In a dream my mother went fishing with her late brother. In that case her soul traveled to the fifth dimension, where the two of them fished in a beautiful environment, reminiscent of the earth plane, that her brother's spirit had created for them there.

Physicists theorize that higher dimensions are very much a part of the universe's reality. "The theory's importance lies in its power to unify all known physical phenomena in an astonishingly simple framework," explains physicist Michio Kaku. Kaku is the author of the widely acclaimed *Hyperspace,* a grand tour of the hyperspace/superstring theory and its implications, and one of the pioneers of the theory of the higher-dimensional universe, a concept that is now one of science's most actively researched. "Everything we see around us, from the trees and mountains to the stars themselves, are nothing but *vibrations in hyperspace.*"

The excitement for all of science lies in the fact that hyperspace theory "may be able to unify all known laws of nature into one theory," Kaku says, and thereby give us "the unification of all known physical forces."

In our three-dimensional world we consider length, width, and breadth each to be a dimension. Scientists now consider time to be a fourth dimension. Time is considered the fourth temporal dimension, and higher-dimensional *space* begins with the fifth dimension. Physical evidence of the fifth dimension, say physicists, may actually be *light,* which can be explained as vibrations in the fifth dimension.

Hyperspace theory goes even further, positing ten basic dimensions, and up to a total of twenty-six. These extra dimensions are spatial dimensions—dimensions of space—that exist beyond the dimensions that we encounter under so-called normal circumstances on the earth plane.

So, what's in that space? Science says an infinite number of parallel universes, which can bleed through into ours (and vice versa) through "wormholes," tunnels of a sort that link space and time. These tunnels also may open the door (at least in theory) for time travel. The fact that this higher-dimensional realm can be described in a physical way by science makes it even easier for us to visualize this realm where we exist as higher vibrational energies—spirits or souls—in the prelife/afterlife.

At present, science says, we can't muster up enough pure, raw energy to transport matter into the higher dimensions. But if matter weren't so dense, if it vibrated at a higher frequency, it could get into higher-dimensional space without the incredible amount of fuel needed to propel solid beings and solid things. Of course, if we didn't bother to take our physical bodies with us, we could travel on the higher-vibrational frequencies we can achieve with our spirits.

As spiritual beings temporarily housed in human bodies, we are capable of interdimensional travel. In fact, *anything* of spirit, of consciousness of any kind, can separate out and travel as mind/spirit. It happens in OBEs, NDEs, dreams, visions, and meditative states. This ability explains the phenomena of clairvoyance, telepathy, and thought transference.

We'll see in the stories that follow just how capable we *all* are of interdimensional travel and communication, both from the three-dimensional earthly plane out to the higher-dimensional realm, and from there to here, whether we're "dead" or alive, for our mind/spirit/soul/consciousness is always alive and mobile. It is eternal.

CHAPTER FOUR

Communication:

A Constant Exchange

It's the most natural thing in the world for all of us to be open to higher-dimensional communication, as you'll see in the stories that follow this section.

You don't need accessories or "smoke and mirrors" to be open to, initiate, or receive guidance and messages. If this looks and sounds simple, that's because it *is*.

The more you realize how natural and effortless this communication can be, the more your experiences will prove the point. You have probably initiated or received communications before, even if you are unaware that your experiences have actually been messages or guidance from the afterlife dimension because you haven't known to label them as such.

To increase your ability to be open to this kind of communication, I offer a few guidelines and tips that can help you create a receptive frame of mind. But, as you'll see in the stories shared here, those now living in the higher dimension find a variety of ways to contact us, even when we're not necessarily open to that contact (primarily because many of us don't believe it's possible), and ultimately it is our *acceptance* of the contact that allows us to understand its purpose and interpret it.

The more consistent we are mentally, spiritually, physically, and emotionally, the more attuned we will be to communication with the afterlife, and the clearer and more accurate we will be in receiving information during this direct, intuitive, transcendental teaching and communicating process.

We must learn to recognize the signs of communication, which include synchronicity, clairvoyance, clairaudience, clairsentience, visible energy forms, dreams, symbols, sense of presence, physical movement of objects, and communication in various levels of heightened awareness and meditative states.

In this chapter, we'll explore the various methods of communication by learning from the experiences of people from all over the country who have been in touch with those in the afterlife. Some of those sharing their stories deliberately set out to initiate or receive communication, and some did not. In each case, the experience left all involved more spiritually aware of the great truth that life goes on once one leaves the body. Everyone involved, no matter what his or her level of intuitive receptivity, felt guided, and in many cases helped with very practical matters. All relished the validation that their relationships with those who have passed on still continue.

To begin, let's look at some of the communication basics.

INITIATING COMMUNICATION

We are often unaware that spirit energy is around us. What we may think is just a hunch, a coincidence, or synchronicity, a thought, a dream, a feeling, is actually a presence and/or message from someone reaching out from the higher-dimension realm. Spirits communicate most often through thought transference. Recognizing that, we can learn to remain open to the guidance of spirit. Spirits cannot be reached constantly or directly at all times, because they are leading lives over there, not constantly hovering over *us*. But, they do get the message eventually, and will attend to us as quickly as they can.

When you are trying to make contact with spirits who passed over, you may find it helpful to create an atmosphere of receptivity by following these suggestions:

- Place yourself in a quiet environment: light a candle, burn incense, play music you know the spirit liked.

- Relax and focus on a feeling of peacefulness.

- Be open to sending and receiving feelings and messages.

- Feel love and goodwill.

- Think of some pleasant moment or something that belonged to the spirit in order to establish contact and an emotional connection.

- Do not use mind-altering drinks or drugs.

- Say silent or audible prayers of any kind that reinforce the desire to have contact for the highest good.

- Meditate.

- Breathe deeply and evenly.

- Listen to quiet instrumental music you like.

- Sit comfortably.

These aren't tips for holding a seance or performing parlor tricks. These are vibration-raising spiritual practices that help to open the pathways of interdimensional communication. Do not expect instant spirit contact, though it may happen in some form. Routinely opening yourself up to any variety of contact paves the way for an ongoing interdimensional relationship with spirit. You may find, for example, that after some time contact is made through dreams, in meditation, by synchronicity, or simply the feeling of presence and guidance.

Once the pathway is opened, it is infinitely easier for those in the afterlife to communicate. They *do* want to communicate, and often we are just not receptive or able to recognize the signs of contact when they appear.

Before long, you won't have to remind yourself consciously to think or do anything special, you'll just always be open to receiving and *recognizing* communication. If you desire communication with a particular spirit at a particular time you may want to initiate it by asking silently or out loud for the specific presence, by taking a few relaxing breaths or creating a loving, receptive mood, by praying, or by requesting communication in dreams before going to sleep.

TWO-WAY COMMUNICATION

When you communicate with anyone, whether that person is here on the three-dimensional earth plane in a physical body, or in spirit in the higher-dimensional afterlife realm, the process is all about interaction and clarity, sending and receiving communication in any format.

You'll want to keep in mind the following important points:

- If for some reason you are blocked, a spirit will often communicate through another psychically receptive person. A person who receives the communication from spirit is called a medium or channeler. Many people you would consider otherwise "ordinary" have this ability. They could be friends, family, or colleagues, not just professional expert intuitives.

- Join with others. There is power in numbers when contacting the afterlife: with one other person or in a group, your consciousness (and therefore your vibration) is raised faster and higher.

- Don't try to force contact with spirits. They may be occupied. Just put out the telepathic "message" and they will receive your request either directly or from other spiritual beings and will respond when it is the right time.

- Spirits *cannot* force *you* to do anything. They cannot override your free will. They can positively influence and guide you. They can impress your mind with ideas, thoughts, or suggestions of a helpful nature, and enable you to make positive decisions and move in the right life direction.

- Once you become comfortable being open to contact you'll find you're more aware of codes from spirit: a smell, a touch, an impression, a symbol, a form, a chill, a light flickering, any number of sounds. These signs can come at any time, even when you're not consciously asking for communication.

- Spirits possess all of the five senses. They feel joy, sorrow, grief, love—the whole range of emotions. They even experience hunger, although food in the afterlife isn't like what we have here. It is a vibrational counterpart of the actual physical substance that does provide satisfaction.

- Spirits most often initiate contact in the dream state because it is more convenient, comfortable, and easily acceptable to people; it isn't startling to see a "deceased" loved one in a dream state. Also, the conscious mind is at rest and the subconscious and

superconscious are very active and open while
dreaming.

- Keep a dream diary. Note what is said and given to
you in symbols.

- Before you go to sleep, ask for clear, concise, direct
information from a spirit and you will generally
receive it in dreams. I'm personally not a big fan of
symbolism; I like my communication to be quite
direct. You can receive so much information from
your dreams and spend as much time as you want,
night after night, meeting with loved ones who are
in spirit. They can even take you on a visit to the
higher-dimensional realm of the afterlife and teach
and show you what they are doing and learning. I
have gone on many trips like this with my mother.
The sights, sounds, colors, and feelings are so
heightened that words cannot express it unless you
experience it as well.

- Spirits will work diligently, especially upon our request, to make events work to your benefit.

- Spirits love it when you keep in contact and recognize their communication. They come to us out of
love, concern, and the desire to communicate the
fact that they are very much alive.

- Spirits have a tremendous sense of humor, too, just
as they may have had when they were on the earthly
plane.

I have learned that there is no reason to fear dying. I know that on our spiritual path here and in the higher dimensions that there is no escaping responsibility, that we experience challenging situations not to overwhelm or depress us but to provide us with valuable lessons. This enables us to overcome anything by using our Higher Power's universal laws of love, faith, perseverance, praise, forgiveness, and compassion.

BUSTING THE MYTHS

Spiritual beings became identified with the ghostly image because their ethereal, transparent forms can sometimes be experienced visually. These energy forms are the basis for the misconception that spirits are cloaked in white, like a costume, when, in fact, spiritual energy is rarely seen.

To straighten out some other misconceptions, keep the following in mind about life in spiritual form:

- We do not get a set of wings when we die. The after-life isn't a place where we're assigned to a cloud and then float around.

- We are not assigned to heaven, hell, or purgatory for x number of years. We will attract a sphere of spirits of similar vibration and evolve from there.

- We do not remain forever as we were when we left the earthly plane. A mean, miserable, selfish person, for example, will eventually evolve to a happier, lighter, brighter being. Since there is no *time* in the higher-dimensional realms, however long this enlightening process takes is not a problem. Since spirits have free will, some will take longer than others.

- Spirits do not "do" things for those on the earthly plane. They help, assist, make impressions, synchronize, harmonize, guide, and send energy.

- We do not get specific clothing in the afterlife, like a heavenly robe. Our spirit clothing reflects our level of spiritual growth and consciousness.

- We can come close to and even pass through those on the earthly plane.

- We can communicate from any distance, directly or through another spiritual being. Communication travels instantaneously through time and space. We move freely just by thinking about it.

- Spirits aren't limited at all by the physical as we are when we're in our bodies.

- There are no evil spirits. On the earthly plane as well as in the higher-dimensional realms, we can attract negative energy only if we are open to it and live in fear. The spiritual power of love and light protects us. Spirit cannot control anyone on the earthly plane in the form of possession, revenge, or anger. Only we can bring these negativities upon ourselves.

HEALING

Spirits can perform healing upon those on the earthly plane, and certainly their power to do so is greater when we actually request it. What they are actually doing is infusing us with positive, loving energy that increases our vibrational frequency, which leads to physical healing. So, we are actually healed by our own energy that has simply been boosted.

ANIMALS

Animals also have spiritual energy, and those who have passed on will often appear to us in our dreams or as visions in a waking state. Animals on the earthly plane greatly sense the presence of spirits and can hear and see them often when we cannot and respond accordingly by making noise or acting out.

CHILDREN

Children who pass on often spend a great deal of time in contact with their loved ones on the earthly plane and are closely guided by other spiritual beings. When children's spirits make contact they may seem older or younger than when they passed on, and may appear to speak more articulately than we might expect of their actual age, as a result of the soul's enlightenment.

RITUAL

Formal communication with the dead by using rituals has long been a part of native cultures, and you may wish to embrace some of these ceremonies if you feel they have special meaning to you. However, rituals aren't necessary for afterlife communication.

When I lived in Japan with Buddhist families, they prayed daily at their home altars to the spirits of relatives, asking for guidance. They prayed for the eternal peace of their ancestors and gave offerings of food, particularly fruits.

If you enjoy the symbolism of ritual, by all means include it in your spiritual life.

AFTERLIFE COMMUNICATION EXPERIENCES

I feel the presence of my mother's spirit so often it's as if she had never left at all. In business, when I'm making a decision, I'll hear her voice giving me advice. She always liked to be the life of the party, so she still accompanies me when I do anything social, in my travels and my spiritual work with individuals and groups. She provides guidance in all areas of my personal life and my spiritual development and pays particular attention to my health. When she was here on the earthly plane she was gifted with an ability to pass on great healing energy, and now she'll come through *my* hands, and I can tell that it's her energy because it feels different from any other energy-boosting experience.

My friend Bob, whom I mentioned in an earlier chapter, worked in the medical field when he was here on the earthly plane. Since passing over as the result of complications from AIDS, he not only assists those in the afterlife who are entering the higher-dimensional realm after passing from AIDS-related illnesses, but he also focuses his earth-plane attention on healing, just as he did when he was here. I always ask for him to be with me when I am dealing with anything medical. I can feel his healing energy, his guidance, and his concern.

My father worked as a golf course greenkeeper here on the earth plane, and nature was his great love. When I'm doing things in the yard, tending flowers or plants, my father's spirit will come through and I find that in his presence I know a lot more about what I'm doing out there!

Like you and me, people all over the country have an ongoing relationship with those who have passed on. Their stories can inspire, teach, and enlighten us.

It is not uncommon for an entire family to be in contact with those who have passed on to the afterlife.

Two very special families share their stories of ongoing relationships with a loved one who is now living in the higher-dimensional realm. The first, a Protestant family in the Midwest, opens this section. The last, a Jewish family in New England, completes it.

They're your average upper-middle-class family in the Midwest: Mom, Dad, a bunch of kids, and a house full of visitors from the afterlife. Grandparents, friends, even dead folks they don't know. This is not a tale of ghosts or things that go bump in the night, though; this is about a family that opened their minds, their hearts, and their souls to communication from those in a higher dimension.

Linda's mother had just come out of a very difficult surgery—one the doctor later admitted to "messing up," Linda says, and it was clear that the 69-year-old woman was nearing her time.

"On the day that she died," says Linda, herself the mother of five, "I sat with her all day, I told her I loved her and said, 'Please try to get in touch with me after you've gone. I'll be open to it.'"

As in so many other cases, afterlife communication began with this simple, heartfelt request.

The night of her mother's funeral, in February 1989, Linda was half asleep when her mother's spirit first appeared.

"I was in a dreamlike state," she recalls. "First I saw darkness, and then the impression of air and movement. Suddenly she was there. She came toward me, and she looked so beautiful and radiant wearing a coat with a high collar. She looked very serious, though. She stood about ten feet away and said, 'Now you have to take care of your father.' I knew it was real. It was different than a dream."

In November of that year, once again Linda's mother came to her in a dreamlike state.

"It was a dark, cloudy afternoon and I fell asleep on the couch," Linda remembers. "It felt so real. I was back at the hospital and my whole family was there in the waiting room, and it was a glorious, radiant day. We knew that we were waiting for something, but we had a peaceful feeling. I was resting on a couch and the next thing I know my mother is waking me up in the waiting room. I was so happy to see her. She leaned over and kissed me and she looked so peaceful and beautiful. I asked her a thousand questions and she answered them all, but I only remember a few of the answers because I had the sense that I'm not supposed to remember all of it, that I'm not to know most of this until I pass over."

When Linda asked her if she was okay, her mother replied, "Yes."

When asked if she'd seen any of her family on the

other side, she also said, "Yes," and added, "I'm with them and they send their love."

What did her mother tell her about the afterlife?

"I asked all about heaven and she told me all about it," Linda continues; "I can't remember any of it, but in the dream I know that I got it all and was satisfied with what she told me and that it now subconsciously guides me.

"She said that she had to go rest and she went back to her hospital room," Linda continues. "She said, 'The doctors made a mistake and I died, but now I'm reborn and everything is fine.'"

With that message, Linda's dream ended.

"I was so full of joy to know she was okay, and still with us in this spiritual way. I knew then that there wouldn't be a complete separation. I wasn't at the stage in my spiritual development where I was ready to believe completely that her spirit would be around, so I wanted to go back to sleep so that I could be with her. Soon, though, I realized that I didn't have to be dreaming to feel her presence."

Linda says that her mother's spirit comes to her often now, "especially when I need ideas or support or help, and because of my openness to this, my so-called psychic abilities are evolving."

In March 1993, Linda's daughter Andrea, then twelve, startled the family by reporting to them that her grandmother was communicating to her from the afterlife.

If felt natural to Andrea, a very bright student who had shown a highly intuitive nature since the age of three. The conversations she had with her grandmother's spirit contained information that she couldn't have known otherwise, and this was verified by other family members.

After that otherwise normal morning, other souls began contacting Andrea; some were family members who had passed on, and some were complete strangers. The family would gather for sessions from time to time, during which Andrea would share what these higher-dimensional presences were telling her about the afterlife, as well as pertinent personal information that the family was once again able to verify.

The appearance of heaven, Andrea was told, was different for each individual.

"I see what their heaven looks like when I'm talking to them," Andrea says very matter-of-factly. "My grandmother was a really good cook and had a garden and loved flowers. Her heaven is a big garden with a tree, and the sun always shines. She walks down a long pathway, and she visits people. She tells me she's learning a lot there, learning how to progress up to the next spiritual level."

After Andrea's brother's sixteen-year-old friend died in January 1994, he appeared to Andrea in her bedroom mirror.

"This was the first time I saw a spirit with my eyes and not just in my mind," Andrea says. "He came, it seems, just to let us know that he was around."

At the beginning, says Linda, "every week the souls of different people would come to visit with Andrea. They were excited by her gift, that there was someone they could communicate with so easily."

Andrea and her family are Presbyterians, and they don't attend church. Until Linda and Andrea began to receive afterlife communications, they didn't give too much attention to things of a spiritual nature other than a belief in a Higher Power or God.

"I'm learning more about life through these experiences," says Andrea, "and how to go with my instincts, how to handle stuff."

Most important, though, Andrea adds shyly, is that she's learning "that I can help people."

At first Andrea's siblings found all of this a bit unusual. Soon they realized how natural it was, and now they, too, have been in communication with the afterlife.

One brother, only ten at the time, started crying one day when he felt a tickling in his stomach. It didn't hurt. "It was the most beautiful thing I've ever felt," he told his mother, Linda.

"What is it?" she asked.

He said it was his grandmother's presence floating through him.

He would later learn that it's commonly believed that when spirit energy "walks through" us, we can either feel it directly or experience another physical reaction such as sneezing, hiccups, burping, mild headache, or, yes, even tickling. These reactions are accompanied by something you don't normally expect to feel when burping or sneezing: a lovely sense of peacefulness.

Friendship stands the test not only of time but of spiritual evolution as well. Our relationships with friends continue when one has moved on to life in the higher-dimensional realm, and can

even intensify as they take on aspects of further enlightenment.

Holly, a journalist in her thirties, tells the story of the sudden departure from the earth plane of a friend and colleague whose guidance and sense of humor persisted from the afterlife, and who found a way to ease the pain she felt at his passing by communicating in a very poignant way.

When the phone rang at seven-thirty one morning in the winter of 1994, I just figured that it was one of my friends touching base before going into work, as they often do. I'm usually up at sunrise, but on this particular morning I had rolled over and gone back to sleep, since I'd been up late writing the night before. In a groggy, half-asleep voice I answered the phone.

"Holly," said my friend Anna, who didn't need to identify herself. "Dan . . . is . . . dead."

Anna could hardly get the words out. Her voice was hollow and shaken by disbelief. She was on the verge of tears.

"What?" I gasped, snapping fully awake at the sheer unbelievability of her words. "Oh my God, what happened?"

She'd just heard the news on the radio. Dan had had a simple cold, or so he thought. It quickly turned into pneumonia. Friends rushed him to the hospital, but it was too late. Massive doses of antibiotics couldn't save him. By late evening he was on life support, and a few hours later he was gone. Within forty-eight hours he'd gone from sniffles to death.

Dan was only forty-seven. He was a well-known, brilliant, insightful writer with a razor-sharp wit. He was sought after for his easy companionship and love of great conversation. He was our friend.

The city was stunned, in mourning. Tributes poured in. We went to Dan's memorial service. We laughed. We cried. His fiancée sat quietly in front. She reminded me of all those movies where Shirley Temple braced herself against sorrow by being the "brave little soldier" her daddy had asked her to be.

There were times in the weeks and months that followed when I felt—is guilty the word?—well, I felt unsettled by my reaction to Dan's death. As if I didn't have the right to mourn him so much. Others had known him far better than I had. But, then again, that could be said about anyone who passes away. There will always be those who know someone better than you do, and those who hardly know him at all. Dan was the kind of man who had a big impact on you no matter where in that spectrum you happened to fit.

Besides being reminded of my own mortality and how unpredictable each day really is, my focus after Dan's death was on what I had learned from him—professionally, creatively, and personally—and how I wished he could know how much I'd appreciated that guidance and those inadvertent life lessons.

When someone dies unexpectedly we rarely get to say good-bye or have any kind of closure at all. Just in case he happened to be listening from the afterlife dimension, I told him everything I wanted him to know.

My first response from him came one afternoon when,

already quite tired from a particularly heavy recent work-load of interviews, research, and writing, I waffled between plowing ahead with my next assignment and taking the rest of the day off and renting a video—one of my favorite ways of clearing my head. I stood in my dining room and stared into the living room directly at the TV. "Well, what's it gonna be," I thought, "head to the video store or back to my desk?" I decided on the desk. Then the video store. Then the desk again. Then the video store. Then the desk. I turned my back to the TV and upon taking my first step out of the dining room I was startled by a soft *thud* behind me.

I turned around and looked back into the living room. Much to my surprise, the TV's remote control had found its way onto the carpeted floor. I know my remote control and it does not have legs. Just two seconds before, it had been in its usual spot on the coffee table. Now it was snuggled into my carpet.

"Okay, okay, Dan," I said aloud. "I get the message!"

I grabbed my keys and my purse and went out the door. Destination: video store. It was Dan, I'd decided instantly, who'd flung my remote. Well, why not? It made perfect sense to me since he'd spent a large portion of his writing career as a film critic. It was as if he were saying to me, "Take a break. Forget the desk. Rent the video."

Not at all alarmed—I'm a veteran of a variety of rather creative and often amusing communications from the after-life—I thanked him for his playful reminder that two hours of movie washing over me was exactly what I needed. I rented a great new film, put my feet up, and got on with the business of relaxing. A couple of months had passed since Dan's passing, and theory has it that those in the afterlife make their presence known in some way to those left behind in a rather orderly manner: family, spouses or significant others, and closest friends first, then the rest of the gang. Although I'd certainly been open to communication from him earlier, he got around to me on his own spiritual schedule.

Once that initial contact was made, I sensed that Dan knew I'd like to keep in touch. By the middle of the summer he'd obviously decided to address my need for closure. He certainly had many, many people to visit, and now it was my turn. I was not expecting my second communication from him but was more than grateful when it happened.

He came to me in a dream, a dream unlike any other I'd ever had because of its uniquely ethereal quality, its gentle, natural *realness*. On a bright, sunny day I stood calmly on the platform of an old-fashioned train station. It appeared as though I had been transported to the nineteenth century, and even the visual quality of the dream seemed antique—everything had a pleasing fuzziness about it, as if a camera lens was ever so slightly out of focus. The air was warm and comforting. The sky was the robin's-egg blue of a picture postcard. The intricately designed and elegant wooden train station was strangely quiet. I realized that I was the only one there, outside or inside.

I knew then why I had come there, and whose train I was waiting for.

Soon a stately, gleaming nineteenth-century steam

engine chugged into the station pulling no more than a half a dozen train cars. It stopped right in front of me and the door to one of the cars opened as if by itself. I knew that I was supposed to step up and into this gorgeous train, which looked like the Orient Express. As I climbed aboard, Dan appeared in front of me in the doorway, perfectly alive and perfectly healthy, his hair the dark brown it had been in his younger days. Although I was wearing something I sensed was classic, though distinctly of the present century, he was dressed for the nineteenth century in a soft, white cotton shirt with no collar flaps but buttoned up to the neck. His sleeves were long and billowy, his pants chocolate brown and loose, like the dress pants of that era. He looked radiant, serene.

We spoke very little, but communicated a great deal telepathically. I knew that the train was Death, and that he was making stops at various stations to say good-bye to people, one at a time. He wasn't sad, but instead quite peaceful.

"I wanted to say good-bye," he said aloud as he ushered me into the train car. I looked around to see banquette seating in crushed burgundy velvet, plenty of polished wood and brass. We stood facing each other, my back to the train station, and he put his arms around me gently and tenderly, giving me a hug that I can barely find the words to describe. It wasn't short, it wasn't long. It wasn't passionate, it wasn't casual. It was deep and peaceful, loving and protective. It was what every last hug should feel like.

He sensed my sadness at having to say good-bye, and telepathically he let me know that he would still be around me, yet in another dimension. He thanked me for my friendship. I thanked him for his. We communicated other feelings in the same telepathic manner as we did these. Finally, I knew that he had to leave. He looked at me and then slowly walked me back to the door. I told him aloud that I would miss him, and he smiled. We had a brief hug, and then I walked back down the steps and stood on the platform and faced him. It was clear to both of us that he was not allowed even to descend the steps, let alone leave the train. He smiled and waved at me. Although I felt sadness, I was not grief-stricken, because he had enveloped me in his sense of peace.

The train began to pull slowly out of the station as I stood motionless on the platform. Dan turned and walked back into the train car, but I could still see him through the side windows of the train for a few more moments. Then his car was far enough from the platform that I could no longer see him and the last car passed slowly by me.

I knew that as soon as the entire train was away from the station it meant that Dan had passed over to the other side. The train leaving indicated his death. I felt him pass over as the train headed further away from the station. It was certain and final, but calm.

It was then that my visual perspective of the dream changed and I was out of the picture, watching myself standing on the station platform, watching as the train's caboose was now just a dot in the distance between the bright green trees.

And then I woke up.

I felt light and warm. A very pleasant, happy feeling, considering that I had just been present at the death of a friend. I moved slowly out of bed, relaxed and alert, though not overly energetic. In fact, I had much the same feeling that I have while sitting on the beach on a quiet day watching the waves gently meet the shore.

Mostly, I felt at peace about Dan's death. We had said good-bye. We each had our closure in such a loving way. And I knew without a doubt that no matter where he was, his spirit would always be around me and everyone else who had known him.

As I write this, it's been exactly one year since Dan's passing. He hasn't done any parlor tricks since flipping my remote control last spring. He hasn't shown up in any other way that I've been aware of, though I'm sure he's keeping an eye on me from time to time. And that dream last summer? I will always think of that as his gift to me, more precious than anything any "living" person could give another.

Some people maintain a relationship with loved ones who now live in the afterlife in quite dramatic ways. Others simply feel guided and loved by a presence that is constant in their daily life.

My sister, Sandra Post, is one of those people, and she has also received afterlife guidance from our mother and father. In fact, she feels as if they have passed on their creative gifts to her from this other dimension. I'll let her tell you how.

My mother and father are always with me. It's as if their spirits have gone into *me*. My father loved gardening, and my mother loved to cook. Since they passed on it's as if they also passed their abilities on to me. I'm a much better gardener and cook since their passing.

When my father died I knew exactly the moment. I felt severe pain in my stomach and chest—out of nowhere—and a feeling of impending doom. When I got back to the hospital, I was told that he had died, and it turned out to be at exactly the moment when I felt that pain.

Six months after my mother died, I felt as if her spirit had entered my body because I found myself humming songs from her era, songs she loved. I'd never done that before. It felt like a message from her. She guides me still with her knowledge and wisdom. I find myself using a lot of her mannerisms and expressions, but the way in which she communicates with me the most often is in the kitchen. I felt her guiding me especially when I cooked for my stepfather who recently passed away. It's like she directed how and what to make for him for dinner in exactly the way she used to prepare it.

I know that a lot of people communicate in dreams, but I feel her presence in my waking hours, not when I'm asleep. It's as if she never left.

You may think because I live my life with great spiritual awareness I am always successful at making contact with my friends and loved ones who are living in the afterlife. But, like everyone else, I, too, need to be reminded of its simplicity sometimes, of the fact that we can often place undue pressure on ourselves.

Just after my mother died, my friend Deborah Rowley was meditating and my mother appeared to her. First Deborah saw her eyes, then her face, then her hair.

"Tell Linda she doesn't have to work so hard," my mother said.

This meant a lot to me because my mother had the most beautiful, piercing, intense eyes and they appeared to Deborah exactly as I had always seen them.

What did my mother's message mean?

I knew right away. I had been trying to make contact with my mother, trying too hard, apparently. She sent me this message through Deborah to show me that communication can be made with ease.

Debbie Rowley, to whom you were introduced in the previous story, is a teacher who also never stops learning. Her spiritual education continues in all aspects of her life, including her travels. On this particular occasion she was contacted by the spirits of people she had never even met, people from a tumultuous time decades ago.

She tells us a tale of spiritual beings still trapped in the pain of history.

While visiting Verdun, France, in 1990 with my husband, I had the most remarkable experience that transcended time.

We were walking through underground barracks that had been used by soldiers during World War II. I was looking at the beds and thinking that the place had the atmosphere of a submarine: very closed in.

Suddenly I began to hear things. My husband and I were two of only a few people touring the barracks. What I was hearing wasn't coming from the others. I was hearing too many voices, and they were speaking in French. I don't speak it, but I began to repeat phonetically to my husband what I was hearing, and he translated the phrases to me.

I was hearing shouts that he said translated into: "Hurry up!" And then there were other phrases about war.

As soon as I went above ground again, the voices stopped.

Later I found out that the Frenchmen had been trapped down there during the war. They tried to get out, but couldn't because the German soldiers pumped in poison gas and killed them.

I was hearing voices from long ago, of soldiers who died in that underground barracks during the war, only I didn't know it until after we left the site.

With the barracks behind us, I suddenly pictured in my mind the letters P, A, and X. A mile down the road we passed a building that looked like some kind of memorial and my husband shouted, "Look!" There on top of the building were the letters PAX. We found out that the building was a mausoleum where World War II soldiers were buried. And *pax*, of course, is Latin for "peace."

Clearly, the souls of those soldiers who were trapped and gassed were not at peace, and after nearly fifty years they could still be heard crying for help.

Debbie has had some of the most dramatic, symbolic, and touching afterlife communication experiences of anyone I've ever known. Here Debbie tells us of a prophetic dream in which her late aunt passed on a musical message that she would never forget.

Back in 1981, my husband and I were camping in Massachusetts, and while sleeping in our tent I had a dream on a Friday night. In this dream, I was singing the Christmas carol "Silent Night" with my aunt, who had passed on eleven years earlier. She was my mother's sister and had lived across the street from us when I was growing up. When my aunt died, her grandson, the only grandchild she lived to see, was only six months old. In my dream, she and I were singing, and although there were lots of people around us, I don't know who they were.

I awoke on Saturday morning, remembering this dream so clearly and wondering what it meant. Later I would find out exactly what it meant. That Saturday, my aunt's grandson, the one who was a baby when she died, passed away. He'd been riding his bike and was hit by a fire truck. From Wednesday to Saturday he'd been in a coma, but I didn't know anything about it because my husband and I were away on our trip. Just a few hours after I awoke from my dream, my aunt's grandson died at only eleven and a half years old. All I could think about was how in my dream we'd been singing the words, "Holy infant so tender and mild, sleep in heavenly peace."

Lastly, Debbie tells us about the most meaningful prophetic message from the afterlife that she has ever received.

My late grandmother, my father's mother, came to me in a dream in the fall of 1986, and in this dream I was standing in a line in a mausoleum that looked very much like a cavern. The side I was on was the side of the living; the other side was blocked off. I couldn't go over there because it was the side of those who had passed on. And there was my grandmother standing on the afterlife side over a coffin.

She was calling my father's name.

"Why are you calling my dad?" I asked her.

She didn't answer.

"Please stop calling for him," I pleaded. "It's not his time."

She didn't hear me, yet I kept pleading with her to stop calling for him.

Six weeks later, although as far as we knew at the time my father was in perfect health, he died suddenly of a stroke.

In my dream I had been shown that his time was coming very soon and that his mother knew it.

Love is not lost when your life partner passes on to the afterlife. While the sadness and grief at losing their physical presence is intense, knowing that they are still present, although in a very different way, eases the pain of physical separation. Knowing

that their love, concern, guidance, humor, and affection are still actively with you makes all the difference in the world.

On the day after Valentine's Day, in 1969, Allan and Patricia Rusinko were married. They had been engaged for a little more than a year, and were deeply in love. They used to laugh about how they were destined to meet, since they figured out that they had crossed paths many times without even knowing it in the years that led up to their eventual meeting, including her cousin's wedding and a mining disaster at which he was present as part of the rescue team and she was assisting as a nurse.

The couple did not have children, and after nearly twenty years of marriage were enjoying a close, comfortable life together in Chesapeake, Virginia, where Patricia continued in nursing and Allan enjoyed a career in civil service with the government. He loved to work in his garden and had created an award-winning landscape around their home. He was a talented craftsman, building beautiful wooden structures into the landscape and stained-glass creations, including sparkling lamps, that decorated their home.

The happiness of that home was shaken badly when Allan was diagnosed with cancer. He was only forty-two. In the four years from his diagnosis to his passing, Allan would go through surgeries, tests, more surgeries, more tests, treatments, and experimental procedures with a fighting spirit that would not let him give up. With her medical knowledge, Patricia took an active role in her husband's care. He continued to work, to enjoy his family, friends, and hobbies, despite losing a lung and a kidney in the course of the ordeal.

In June 1989, during the operation to remove his lung, Allan "died" briefly and had a classic Near Death Experience in which he saw his late parents and Patricia's father, who had also passed on.

"They were standing there waiting for me," he told Patricia, after his surgery, "but they didn't say anything."

It was not his time to pass over. And because of this experience, something in Allan changed.

"He wasn't afraid to die anymore." Patricia recalls.

Allan's battle with cancer continued for almost three more years. On Saturday, May 23, 1992, at 5 A.M., Allan and Patricia knew that his passing was near.

"We said our good-byes," Patricia remembers, "and the last thing he said was that he loved me."

On a morphine drip for the pain, Allan soon left all pain behind as he lapsed into a coma.

At 2 P.M. Allan passed on with Patricia at his side.

But, in the weeks, months, and years that followed, it became clear to Patricia, her family, and friends that although Allan's body was now considered dead, his soul, his presence, had not died at all. It had simply gone somewhere else, and was able, from time to time, to make heartwarming and amusing visits.

Allan chose as his primary form of communication from the afterlife the radios in the home he had shared with his wife, and communicated most often around special dates that had meant something to the couple.

"It began one night when my mother was visiting and

sleeping in the guest room that Allan had also used as a lit-tle home office," Patricia says. "I think this first visit was his way of saying good-bye to my mother because he hadn't had the chance to do that before he died. In the middle of the night, his radio came on, and it woke my mother up. This was *not* a radio that had any kind of timer on it. The radio was tuned to his favorite station, one that played songs from the seventies and a lot of oldies from the sixties that were our favorites when we were dating."

Six months after Allan had passed on, Patricia needed to get away and went on a cruise with friends. On Novem-ber 22, 1992, the anniversary of their engagement, Allan managed to give his wife a present from the afterlife.

"I had never played roulette before," she remembers. "I bet on his birthdate and won with odds that were thirty-five to one. Then I bet on our wedding anniversary date and also won. I ended up winning one hundred seventy-six dollars on the twenty-fifth anniversary of our engagement."

Patricia began to look into the phenomenon of after-life communication. "I learned that those with a strong commitment like ours often had a hard time letting go of each other."

Allan was going to stick around awhile and make fre-quent appearances until each of them had worked through the grieving process.

The next time he showed up was when Patricia was sitting at his desk at home filling out more of the dozens of insurance and medical papers that remained to be dealt with after her husband's illness and passing.

"I would go into one particular drawer in his desk all

the time, and this time, not long after the cruise, and just about one week before Christmas, I found fifty dollars in cash in the drawer. I know that I had never seen cash in there before. It was as if Allen were giving me a Christmas present."

One month later, in January 1993, the radio on Allan's desk at home turned on, filling the room with their favorite music. This time, although Patricia tried to turn it off, the radio would not stop.

"Finally," Patricia says, "I gave up, stepped back, and it turned itself off! I know it was Allan letting me know that he was around because that day the security system in the house was being worked on, and it was as if Allan had been overseeing everything and letting me know that he was still keeping an eye out for me."

The following month, on February 15, 1993, the day that would have been their twenty-fourth wedding anniversary, Patricia went out to dinner with a girlfriend. Back home alone with her dog, Patricia was sitting in the living room around midnight when she heard a hard knock on the front door. The dog barked wildly. Patricia went immediately to the door.

"No one was there or in the street."

She didn't sleep well that night, and in the morning she turned on the television to the morning news and went into the kitchen to make coffee.

"I had put the remote control on the coffee table, and I was talking to my mother on the phone, telling her that since I hadn't slept well I would probably go back to bed soon for a nap. All of a sudden, the television went off. It had never done that before. I turned it back on. Allan used to signal that it was bedtime by using the remote to turn off the television. Since I hadn't slept well, I figured it was Allan gently suggesting that I should go in for that nap! I had the TV checked out later and there was nothing wrong with it."

Eventually, Patricia began to go out on dates. Allan apparently didn't approve of her first two dating choices.

"Each one of them had taken me out to dinner, and each one had brought me a rose. I had put each in a vase on the television and the next morning found that the petals had fallen off both times."

Around the first anniversary of Allan's death, Patricia and her mother went on a trip to Nashville, and a neighbor watched Patricia's house and the dog.

"Allan used to talk to these neighbors from our deck all the time," Patricia says. "And when I came back from Nashville, my neighbor said she had something to tell me."

The neighbor was hesitant at first, but finally came out with it.

"She told me that she had heard Allan's voice twice outside while I was away," Patricia says. "After she told me that, I shared with her some of the experiences I'd been having."

Patricia also spoke to her Lutheran pastor, who at first clung to his traditional beliefs about heaven and hell, but later on began to open up to the possibility that there was more to death than met the eye.

Not long after her Nashville trip, Allan came to Patricia in a dream for the first time.

"I dreamed I heard something in the hall, and then I saw the blurry figure of a man nearing my bed. As he got closer and clearer, I realized it was Allan," she remembers. "He got into bed with me and lay down next to me. He looked exactly as he did when I'd last seen him, when he died in the hospital. He even had an IV tube hanging from his chest! He looked happy and content, and I laid my head on his chest and said, 'I am *so* happy to see you.' He was smiling, but he didn't say anything. We lay there for a while, then he got up, found his favorite shorts that he used to wear when he was working around the house—I had thrown them away right after he died—and he put them at the bottom of the bed and then disappeared."

With that, Patricia woke up.

"The dream felt so real," she says. "I felt like I had touched him, felt the hair on his chest. I was in a tizzy for three days because it *felt so real*."

Patricia asked around and learned that this had been a very special gift that those in the afterlife can give us. "They have to muster lots of energy to do this," she was told.

On September 23, 1993, sixteen months to the day since he died, Allan again came to Patricia in a dream.

"I dreamed I was in a public building and was paged to answer a phone. I picked up the phone and heard Allan's voice," she recalls.

"I said, 'Allan, is that you?'

" 'Yes,' he replied.

"I asked him, 'Where are you?'

" 'I'm not sure,' he answered, 'but I'm all right and I want you to know that I'm okay. Don't worry.' "

Patricia had received a classic message from the afterlife.

"That startled me awake," she remembers. "After that I was told by people that Allan wanted me to know that he was all right and that I could move on, that I had to stop grieving."

One year later, in September 1994, Patricia met a special man with whom she is now having a committed relationship. He, too, has given her roses, but unlike the others, these flowers have not lost their petals.

"The petals have stayed on for almost three weeks in some cases," she laughs. "I think Allan likes him as much as I do."

Sometimes, spirit energy can infuse us with creative inspiration never before present in our lives and the guidance to transform it into beautiful works of art and music.

"It had been a rotten day," Dorothy Phillips remembers, "and I came downstairs at three in the morning and sat at the piano. The melody just came. In just forty minutes I wrote a rhapsody I called 'A Lover's Dream.' I felt like I'd been guided. I heard messages instructing me on the melody and the chords."

It was more than thirty-five years ago, and although many musicians feel guided spiritually while they compose, whether they're professionals or amateurs, whether they've been playing for many years or are just beginners, that instance felt higher-dimensional to Dorothy.

"The guidance is very definite, and I get even more powerful direction when I write gospel music," she says. "And I find it so strange that I write gospel!"

One of her most recent gospel compositions, "There Is a Mighty Light," was performed in the fall of 1994 by the choir of the Second Presbyterian Church in Fort Lauderdale. You might be tempted to assume that Dorothy is an African-American woman raised in the church, who, moved by spirit, expresses herself in song, but you would be wrong. Dorothy is white, has never affiliated herself with organized religion, although her family is Protestant, and in childhood she decided that a one-on-one relationship with a Higher Power was more to her liking than any one particular religious doctrine. She has also never studied music. She taught herself to read notes, and plays very simply.

Why and how is she guided?

"I step over and I wait for the contact," she explains, "whatever and whoever it is. I believe that we can step out of this particular consciousness and listen to the Universal Mind, just let it come to us with information and guidance."

When that guidance comes, Dorothy says, "it's physical, it's emotional, it comes flowing out."

Her guidance added painting to Dorothy's creative repertoire in 1972, when her second husband, Charles Epstein, whom she still refers to as "my dear Charles," died in middle age after only five years of marriage.

Charles had been an entrepreneur, and "very much

into the arts," Dorothy says. "He had some Lautrec originals and then sold them, but kept copies. He loved Lautrec."

After he passed away, Dorothy, then living in Pennsylvania, began to paint Lautrec re-creations. That was highly unusual, considering the fact that Dorothy Phillips had never painted before nor shown any inclination toward that kind of artistic expression.

Once again, she felt guided. This time, however, she distinctly felt the guidance of her late husband, Charles, and some unnamed spiritual presence that instructed her on the precise colors she should use, the strokes to use, the shadings, every painter's nuance.

Her re-creations were so good, so accurate, that they have been exhibited in galleries across the country and are listed as reproductions with Sotheby's, the prestigious auction house.

When Dorothy moved to Fort Lauderdale, she continued her composing and painting, then added another newfound talent—writing. Again, with no previous interest or training, Dorothy felt guided in her creative expression and enjoyed a new career writing for local publications, primarily covering the social scene.

Today, Dorothy is working on a three-act musical comedy and more gospel numbers. She hopes one day to hear her rhapsody performed by a symphony in Carnegie Hall. "Every composer's dream," she says, laughing.

As for her ongoing higher-dimensional contact, Dorothy likes to quote Edgar Cayce, who described the Universal Mind this way: "A vast river of thought flowing through eternity, fed by the collective mental activity of mankind since its beginning. You can feed into it and draw from it if you develop your own psychic facilities to this degree."

Afterlife communication has helpful, practical aspects, and those who use their spiritual abilities not only personally but professionally to teach, guide, and counsel others are often called upon to relay communication for very practical reasons. Along the way, they also end up providing spiritual lessons as well.

Rick Fawcett, Janon Allegre, and Monnica Sepulveda, three expert intuitives with great compassion, integrity, and wisdom, have much to teach us from their communication experiences on behalf of their clients as well as in relation to their own spiritual lives.

Professional intuitive counselor Frederick "Rick" Fawcett is among the many whose gifts include the ability to make contact with those who are now in the afterlife.

He once made contact on behalf of "a woman who lost her husband in a very tragic way," he recalls. "During the reading I was able to give her information about properties and business that she did not have previous knowledge about."

As is common in other such readings given by psychically gifted people around the world, this California man was able to pass on valuable knowledge to his client.

"I got the information directly from her late husband, from the afterlife. He identified himself with specifics that would only be known to her. As it turned out, she would have lost a lot of money if I hadn't given her the messages that I received from him."

"I'm the most skeptical psychic you'll ever meet," says Janon Allegra, a former real estate broker in her early forties who lives in Nevada, "even though I've had remarkable experiences all of my life."

At eleven, she woke up in the middle of the night to the presence of her great-grandmother. "She came to say good-bye," Janon recalls. "And the next day she died."

In years to come, Janon says she would "write messages to people I didn't even know. These messages were given to me by their loved ones who'd passed on. I was told who to give them to, and as it turned out the information would be very healing for them."

Now, she says, she spontaneously receives messages while giving general psychic readings for clients, messages from the afterlife. "And, often, if their deaths have involved pain, like the trauma of an accident, I can feel the pain."

Skepticism for her and her clients is always dissolved by the accuracy of the information she receives from the afterlife dimension.

"I've gotten information about things that were hidden," she says. "Very often it's papers the deceased want taken care of, especially if the death was sudden and no one had the chance to prepare practical matters."

She recalls one reading for a woman in her eighties.

"Her husband's spirit told me about some money that he'd hidden in their wall heater. So she went and had someone take it apart for her, and sure enough, the money was there. Being able to communicate with the afterlife is very rewarding for me because the information resolves a lot of practical and emotional issues."

How does Janon receive messages from those who have passed on?

"I can see in my mind the people and the information. Often I'll see what looks like a series of photographs, and I'll be able to hear voices," she explains. "And there's always a wonderful feeling of peace and love. Often I can tell someone which other deceased people were waiting on the other side to meet their loved one who passed on."

Given the accuracy of her information, even the most skeptical clients have come away from readings emotionally uplifted, reassured, and with greater understanding of life's many dimensions.

"Our lessons do continue in the afterlife," she says, "and I've learned that messages can come to people from perfect strangers as well as loved ones and friends. Usually it's practical information that they want to pass on. Someone who's passed on who worked in their career field will come through with practical advice. I've even received messages like, 'Call so-and-so because it's important to your job.'"

Reincarnation theory holds that those who die very young, suddenly, or violently, will often reincarnate sooner than others, and Janon has received confirmation of this from the afterlife.

"A few Vietnam vet spirits have told me that they

have already reincarnated within their families as nephews, nieces, and others born soon after their deaths.

Like others who communicate with the afterlife, Janon has also seen and been told about the spiritual effects of suicide.

"Those who commit suicide experience intense emotional pain in the afterlife," she cautions. "It is not the answer to dealing with life's issues. Watching their spirits watch their own funerals is just awful."

Monnica Sepulveda's intuitive gifts have enabled her since childhood to receive information from the afterlife dimension and communicate with the souls, essences, or spirits who inhabit that realm.

"We still continue our relationships with people after they've passed on," she reminds her clients as well as the general public when she makes media appearances. "We need to learn how to tap into our intuition and the higher frequencies so we can each communicate with the afterlife. Because in the spirit world you can go anywhere with thought, those who've passed on have the ability to communicate with us in this dimension, not just each other in their dimension. And *anyone* here can participate."

Based in Aptos, California, near San Francisco, Monnica focuses on "helping people with relationships by communication with afterlife family and friends," she explains, adding that she stresses "the importance of personal empowerment, especially for women."

By guiding people through communication with those in the afterlife, Monnica helps them resolve personal issues, learn spiritual truths, and see themselves as unlimited spiritual beings who are connected to everyone and everything in the multidimensional universe.

"When we pass on, we have a Life Review that shows us not only what we've experienced in the life we just left, but what other people have gone through, too. We can feel how they've felt. Anyone whose life we touched in any way. You'll be able to feel the joy and love someone felt because of you and also all the hurt or injustice you ever caused," she reminds us. "But, people need to learn to do this on a regular basis while we're still here and not wait until we die and have a Life Review in the afterlife. Empathy is the best lesson in communication, and most people aren't aware of how we affect other people. I wish we could have a Life Review each night, perhaps in our dreams, to see how we've affected everyone during our day. We can learn from what goes on in the afterlife, and we should apply those lessons to our lives here before we pass on."

The body-mind-spirit connection has withstood the rigorous scientific study and testing of modern medicine, with a new branch of medicine emerging: psychoneuroimmunology. The principles that we are finally able to describe in scientific terms have nonetheless been operating for millions and millions of years, since life here first began, since time began, however we want to describe the energy, or life force.

One of Monnica's personal lessons from a spiritual dimension showed her the power we all have to heal.

"I was only twelve years old when this happened," she recalls. "One night I heard the very loving voice of a woman speaking to me. When I was five I'd had eye surgery to correct what they call 'lazy eye,' and I was wearing glasses. The voice told me to say an affirmation for one year and that if I did that my eyes would heal. I still remember the words, more than thirty years later."

Each day, Monnica would recite her healing affirmation:

I see through the eyes of God,
for God is within me and we are one.
God's vision is perfect,
and my vision is perfect,
and for this I give thanks today.

"One year later, I had perfect vision," Monnica remembers. "And I threw my glasses away. Today I have twenty–twenty-five vision, better than 'perfect' twenty-twenty."

The ethereal voice told Monnica that this kind of affirmation would work on any part of the body.

"Since we're more aware now and we're vibrating at a higher frequency, affirmations work even more quickly now," she says. "So, it probably wouldn't have taken a full year if this were to happen today."

Monnica has also received messages for special occasions, one of which she was asked to relay six years ago.

"My cousin, who had died while in her twenties, came to me while I was mediating one Thursday in August 1989," says Monnica. "I heard her voice from the afterlife, and she said: 'Tell my mother I love her, Happy Birthday, and that I send her white flowers.'"

Monnica didn't know when her cousin's mother's birthday was, so she asked her own mother to find out. Her mother called the woman a week later.

"My mother called my cousin's mother and asked her when her birthday was," Monnica recalls. "And she told her that it had been the previous Thursday, the very day I received the birthday message."

Monnica was giving a reading to a woman whose husband had passed over to the nonphysical realm a few months earlier.

"He gave me important information about their insurance," Monnica says, "and I told her about it."

As in many readings of this nature, the information proved to be correct and quite useful to the man's widow, but that's not what Monnica remembers most clearly about this particular reading.

"During the reading I saw an image of the man standing behind his wife, holding a rose and kissing her on the cheek," Monnica recalls. "So, I told her what I saw. She was so touched by this because, as she told me, every Friday her husband would come up from behind her, hand her a rose, and kiss her on the cheek."

Monnica has consulted with law-enforcement officials as well as private citizens when asked for guidance from spirit in order to locate a missing person, solve a crime, or clear up a mystery.

Like many other expert intuitives, Monnica donates her time when asked to help find someone who has disappeared. In this case, she tells us about the extraordinary spirit guidance that solved a tragic mystery.

In September 1990, I was contacted by three friends of a man. They were concerned because he was missing from a camping trip they'd taken in the woods.

The afterlife communication I received was from the man's grandmother, who was now in spirit. She told me that he drove a red truck, that he chewed tobacco, had a brother who'd passed on, wore Pendleton clothes, and was despondent over a broken romance.

All of this was confirmed later by his friends and family.

The grandmother's spirit also told me that his friends wouldn't be able to find his mother. And, yes, they confirmed that, too. They'd been trying to reach her and were unable to. Later we learned that his mother had been on vacation.

During this reading, his grandmother told me what had happened to her missing grandson, and unfortunately it was what no one ever wants to hear when they're concerned about a missing person: he was dead. She said that he'd committed suicide by shooting himself in the head and was now buried under a light layer of newly fallen snow. She said that his body could be found just northwest of the campsite, and she gave me the latitude and longitude of the location.

Two days after the reading, the body of their missing friend was found within a mile of the location I'd been given, in the snow and with a self-inflicted gunshot wound in his head.

When the spirit of a loved one cannot make contact because the person on the earthly plane doesn't know how to interpret the communication or is otherwise emotionally blocked from opening up to receiving spirit energy, the spirit will often come through to one whose vibrations are high enough to receive it. This is very common, and often once the message is relayed, the knowledge that afterlife communication is real enables the previously blocked person to open up to receiving communication energy.

"One night, a young woman came to me in a dream," says Jill Hearn, a 35-year-old mother of two who lives near Tampa, Florida. "She handed me a red rose."

The young woman was very specific about what Jill was to do with the flower.

"She told me to hand it to Lisa, a woman I had only recently met and had only spoken to maybe twice," Jill recalls.

"Tell her that this is for the best mom in the whole world," said the young woman, who Jill sensed was Lisa's 23-year-old daughter, Lorraine, who had died six months earlier. "And tell her happy Mother's Day."

Having known Lisa only a short time, Jill had never met her late daughter or seen her photo. She also didn't know how Lisa would react to this astounding communication. Nevertheless, Jill did as the young woman in the dream had asked.

She gave Lisa a red rose and told her about the dream.

"Lorraine said to tell you: 'This is for the best mom in the whole world. Happy Mother's Day,'" Jill said as she handed Lisa one perfect red rose.

Lisa's response was both startling and heartwarming: startling because it confirmed that Lorraine had indeed been communicating to Jill from the afterlife, and heartwarming because it went a long way in soothing some of Lisa's intense grief at the loss of her daughter.

"Every year," Lisa told Jill, "Lorraine would give me one red rose on Mother's Day and tell me that I was the best mom in the whole world."

This was the first Mother's Day since Lorraine had passed away, and from the afterlife she managed to send a rose and a loving message to her mother by contacting Jill, a spiritually receptive new friend of her mother, in a dream.

"I was merely a delivery person," Jill jokes. "But that opened Lisa to working through the sadness of losing her daughter because she realized that she hadn't really *lost* her at all. Lorraine was still around, but living now in the afterlife."

After making this very special Mother's Day delivery, Jill saw a photo of Lorraine for the first time, and yes, she looked exactly like the young woman in her dream.

When a parent passes away a child often internalizes the pain, loss, and confusion. The event can produce a lifetime of emotional reverberations if not properly integrated into the child's psyche.

Juanita, a successful artist with her own graphic design company in the Southeast, experienced a spiritual awakening a few years ago that included a very dramatic and sensitive reunion with her father, who had passed away when she was a young child. Here she tells us about their meeting, and how she is now finally able to resume their relationship.

Each year for the past twenty-seven years, I have had a secret wish for Father's Day: to talk face to face with my dad. Over the years I have thought about all the things I have wanted to say and questions I have wanted to ask but never had the chance to. I have imagined him holding me and imagined feeling the coziness I used to feel between us when I was small and would sit on his lap while he drank tea, drew elaborate pictures and typographic designs directly onto our kitchen table top, or when I'd just cuddle up with him each evening in the burgundy overstuffed chair in the living room. I'd stretch my skinny arm around the back of his waist and feel like the safest and most loved little girl on the planet. The only problem with my wish is that I've always known it could never be fulfilled.

My father died suddenly in January 1967, one day before my ninth birthday. He was fifty. I've never allowed anyone to know just how much I really missed him until this past year.

Prior to his death, I remember us spending a lot of time together. I have a wealth of memorable stories that now live in a warm and vivid place in my heart. I felt like we shared a special closeness that didn't need many words. I was content just to be near, watching him in his day-to-day life. It seemed like he could do anything. He had plants growing in the garden, like cotton, which wasn't supposed to thrive in that part of the country, but it did. He raised bullfrogs from pollywogs and then kept them in the downstairs bathtub for two years. He studied them and even wrote an unpublished book about them. I watched him draw and knew that he designed and built all the scooters, bicycles, trailers, and little cars and go-carts that were part of my childhood.

Each autumn, he and his older brother would get together to make red wine. I remember crate after crate of dark blue grapes being carted down our steep basement stairs. I was too small to actually witness this event, but it seemed like the makings of some sort of Italian magic potion.

My dad fascinated me. He brought life in a quirky sort of way to our entire family.

I never placed much importance on my father's death and its effect on my life. I tucked it away under the category of "something unfortunate that happened when I was a kid." It felt as though I put all those unexpressed feelings, words, and emotions into a little invisible jar and screwed the cap on tightly. As long as no one came along to bother the jar, it stayed tucked away and my life seemed at ease. The problem, though, is that I couldn't keep it tucked away forever because people *did* come along to disturb it.

Finally, more than twenty-eight years after his death, my father and I did have that conversation that I'd needed for so long. During a meditation, I was guided back to the last memories I have of my father. I could see my family sitting around our kitchen table, talking. My father came home from work and went to lie down for a while. Later, he came out to the kitchen and then walked into the bathroom. Someone said he was hemorrhaging and needed to get to the hospital. During the days he spent there, I knew he was very sick and had undergone a major stomach operation. Then someone called our house from the hospital. My sister took the call and began to cry.

I knew my dad had died before anyone actually told me. I had a feeling that he had left, but that he was okay now. Looking back, it always seemed more like he disappeared than died because he looked so healthy the last time I saw him.

During the meditation, I saw myself as that little 8-

year-old girl. I knew my father had something important to tell me. This would be the good-bye that we never got to have. I found myself face-to-face with him. He looked healthy and energetic and was casually dressed in new clothes. He looked down at me with a big smile as if he had been waiting for a long time to see me. When I looked up at him I felt excited. He bent down and lifted me up into his arms. I rested my body on his hip. It felt familiar, cozy, and safe. We just looked at each other and hugged for a little while before he began to speak.

"You know it's time for me to go now," he said gently but directly.

"I know," I replied, looking into his eyes. I wasn't sad, and neither was he. I felt as if I understood all along where he was going.

"I have to go on to do more of my work. I came to this family to show you how to live, how to love and be open to all people. Do you understand?"

"Yes."

"Now I need to leave, and it's your turn to carry on this work. Do you understand?"

"Yes."

He looked intently into my eyes. I could feel the connection between us that had always been there, but it became even stronger.

"It only took you eight short years to learn what I came here to teach you about loving people and touching their lives," he continued. "I could not teach you by telling you. I could only teach you by showing you my example. We all have problems along the way, and some will be big, but do not have fear, do not worry about them. They are only tests and you will grow stronger because of them."

He had messages about some of my other family members, about my mission in life, and then he finished by saying, "Keep your life simple. I will watch you grow. You will do well."

He bent down and with one arm gently placed my feet back on the floor. I was satisfied and ready to go and so was he. He had told me all that he wanted me to know and all I needed to hear. He stood up and watched me as I said good-bye and walked out of the room. I knew that meant that he was gone and I understood why.

I know now that my father is always there for me and that I can talk to him at any time. He will listen as I take each step in life. When he left this world the day before my ninth birthday, in many ways if felt like a clock inside me had stopped. When I spoke to him during that meditation, and he spoke to me, it was as if my clock began running again.

Interdimensional relationships aren't limited to just the human spirit. Animal spirits often continue their relationships with us from the higher-dimensional realm.

In a classic example of afterlife communication from a beloved pet, we learn that even man's—or woman's—"best friend" wants us to know that life continues after the body's physical death.

South Florida–based harpist Elyktra has had remarkable intuitive and psychic gifts since early childhood, has studied the field intensively, and leads her life with great spiritual guidance.

Despite the many communications she has received from people in the afterlife, the event that has made the most impact on her was the late-night visit from a beloved nonhuman friend. The young woman was astounded.

"My dog Snowvanya, a beautiful Samoyed, died about eight years ago," she recalls with tenderness and affection in her voice. "Two years later some friends said that they'd seen her out in front of my house."

Not long after, Snowvanya made her presence known to Elyktra.

"One night, around three o'clock in the morning, I heard her nails clicking on the tile floor," she remembers. "It woke me up, and I opened my eyes, looked up, and saw her standing in my bedroom doorway. I suppose I shouldn't have been shocked, given what I know about the afterlife dimension, but I was. I screamed and leaped up!"

Snowvanya made similar return visits every few nights for the next week, perhaps, Elyktra believes, to remind us that where people go, so do pets, and that if human energy is capable of continued interaction with our dimension after that human has passed over to the afterlife dimension, then so is other animal energy.

"These other dimensions—etheric realms—are like Grand Central Station," Elyktra says, laughing. "*Every* kind of spirit hangs around there."

Sometimes, a message from the afterlife takes on a unique physical feeling. Marilyn Sunderman, an internationally renowned painter who makes her home in Sedona, Arizona, and also lectures on the spiritual aspects of creativity, recounts how she received a spirit communication for a friend in an experience that enabled her to sense physically the spirit's previous human form.

One evening, lying in bed, I closed my eyes and felt the presence of a very gentle soul. I pictured white light wrapping around my body for spiritual protection, and I relaxed and opened up to whatever message this spirit might have for me.

Very soon, my body began to feel as if it were changing shape. My hourglass frame soon felt short and stocky. My shoulders felt narrower, my waist lifted higher. Most curious, though, was that a sensation began in my leg—it felt like a part of it was *missing*. The lower part of my right leg, beneath my knee, felt as if it was not there.

Soon a voice flowed through my head.

"Please give a message to my daughter," she said.

I replied that I would, and more words flowed inside my ear.

"Tell her we *live*," she continued.

The message was so simple it startled me.

When it ended, I felt my body's shape return to its normal state.

I called my friend—the daughter the voice spoke about—and asked her to dinner. I let a couple of hours of chitchat go by before I cleared my throat and said, "I have something I'd like to share with you."

How would she believe me? How was I going to have her think I was still sane and credible? I knew that she had a sense of her own spirituality and a desire to learn more, but I didn't know how open she was to the possibilities of the afterlife.

I realized that if I could describe her mother to her, whom I'd never seen and knew nothing of, and if the description was accurate, I would have some credibility.

She nodded *yes* to each part of the description I gave her of her mother. Finally, I told her that there was one last thing about her mother, something I found strange, and maybe unbelievable, and I told her about the sensation I had of the right leg missing below the knee.

"Yes," my friend replied simply. "My mother was a diabetic and had had part of her leg amputated before she passed away."

We stared at each other and I gave her her mother's message:

"We *live*."

Tears flowed down her cheeks.

"Thank you," she said softly. "I needed to know that."

In this last story, we meet a New England family linked not only by their so-called normal familial relationships but also by a most amazing, tender, and even amusing bond with one of them who now resides in the afterlife and communicates with them regularly.

Julie, a writer in her late thirties who lives in the Southeast, tells us about her late uncle, a Connecticut businessman who has never left her life or the lives of his immediate family. This saga spans sixteen years and intertwines the lives of nearly a dozen people whose communication involves dreams, thought transference, telepathy, physical contact, coincidence and synchronicity, clairaudience, clairsentience, the movement of physical objects, energy shifts . . . virtually every interdimensional communication method you can think of.

It is, therefore, a most complete way to finish our look at communication in action.

Julie begins the story with her uncle's death, an event many might say is the end of a relationship. But, as we see, it was merely a step in the continuation of life.

When my uncle Arthur died in April 1978, his entire extended family was not only grief-stricken but in shock.

Arthur, a strong, kind, generous man, was only fifty-three, and shortly before he died, he'd been given the proverbial clean bill of health from his doctors after his annual physical. He had no history of heart disease, no current symptoms, no conditions or irregularities that foreshadowed the sudden massive and fatal heart attack that ended his life here on a sunny spring afternoon.

Although there was no warning, Arthur died exactly as he'd wanted to die. Years earlier, when Bing Crosby died while playing golf, Arthur had announced, "That's how I want to die, too."

He got his wish.

Arthur loved golf, which he had played regularly for many years. On this particular day, the day after his wife's birthday, he keeled over in the middle of his golf game. He simply hit the ground dead.

He was rushed to the hospital, but could not be revived.

As family members were notified in person and by phone, each and every one around the country had the same reaction: disbelief and heart-wrenching sadness. Arthur was a man who was not only loved but *liked* by all who knew him.

I had last seen him two months earlier when he and my aunt were in town for a visit. I was in my early twenties then and finishing college. I was home visiting my parents. Arthur had always been like a second father to me, and I felt a protectiveness from him and the kind of support a father shows a daughter, so when he passed away I grieved as though I had lost a father.

After the funeral, the family gathered at his daughter's home, and I kept expecting Arthur to walk in at any moment. Everyone there said the same thing. Dozens and dozens of family members from all over the country were all together as if for any other special occasion—a wedding, a bar mitzvah—so where was Arthur? Where was the sturdy man with the pigeon-toed walk, the one who always filled the room with the warm, fragrant, comforting smell of his pipe tobacco?

I'm sure he was there. It was just that we couldn't see him. In fact, although many other family members had passed on before him, most of them quite a bit older,

Arthur's presence continued to swirl around everyone who was close to him in a way that no one else's ever had, no matter how much they were loved and missed. And it remains that way to this very day.

It is said that when someone dies suddenly and those left behind have a difficult time accepting his passing, the spirit is more likely to maintain contact, as if to help give comfort and to remind us that he is still with us, though in another dimension, another form. If that is so, then Arthur's spirit behaved as a textbook case!

I've often wondered where Arthur found the time to tend to his spiritual growth and duties in the afterlife, because he kept in such close contact with so many of us after his death.

My aunt, of course, experienced some of the most dramatic incidents of contact. Not long after Arthur died he make one of many appearances at their Connecticut home. Although he was never seen, he made sure that physical clues were left, and in this particular instance the clue took the form of golf-shoe prints imbedded deeply in the carpet between the upstairs hall closet in which he kept the shoes and the window opposite it.

My aunt was able to rule out practical joking because no one had been in the house with her on the day the foot-prints appeared and the golf shoes were no longer in the house.

Arthur's visits to his daughter were also quite classic. She could smell his vanilla pipe tobacco and feel his presence often in her home. No one in her home smoked and she didn't allow visitors to light up.

"I always felt that when I could smell his tobacco it was his way of letting me know that he was watching over me," she told me, only after I confided in her about my contact with him. Like many people when the conversation turns to such things, she was hesitant to talk about her experiences with anyone who might make light of them. I understood how she felt because I had waited sixteen years before telling *her* about how her father had remained in regular contact with me ever since his death, although I had been sharing my experiences with my aunt from the very beginning.

A few months after Arthur died, he made his presence known to me for the first time. Early on a Sunday morning I stood in the bathroom wearing a terry-cloth robe and leaned into the shower to turn the water on. A cool breeze wafted through the room, which was strange, since the door and window were both closed and the air conditioner wasn't on. That certainly got my attention, though I didn't know what to make of it. I wasn't scared, just puzzled. But the puzzle was solved a moment later when I felt the gentle touch of a hand on my shoulder and heard my uncle Arthur's voice calling my name aloud. I was startled, but not spooked, since spiritual or metaphysical experiences had always been part of my life and were, therefore, the norm to me. Still, the unmistakable directness of this contact left me speechless as I slowly left the bathroom and walked back down the hall to the living room, where my roommate was having a cup of coffee and reading the Sunday paper.

"My uncle Arthur just made a visit from the great beyond," I said casually.

"You mean the one who died?" she asked, looking only mildly surprised. "Where?"

"In the bathroom," I replied in a tone that implied that spirits visit bathrooms every day. "I was about to get into the shower."

I told her the rest, and as I finished, the phone rang. She got up and answered it. Then all the color drained out of her face as she came back into the living room and told me that the caller was a guy she barely knew, someone from one of her classes whom she'd been in a study group with and who also had spiritual interests. He wanted to talk to me, she said. I'd heard her end of the phone conversation from the living room and all she'd said was "Hello."

"I don't know him," I said, "so why does he want to talk to *me?*"

"When I answered the phone," she explained, "he said he was calling because he sensed that my roommate had a spirit in her energy field."

"I guess I'd better talk to him," I replied quickly, not knowing whether to laugh, scratch my head in disbelief, or feel relief at the instantaneous assistance.

I went to the phone and we spoke for only a few minutes. He told me what I had already suspected, that my uncle had shown up to comfort me, but that my intense sadness at his passing was keeping him too closely bound to the earth plane.

"He won't be able to go on and do what he has to do until you begin to let go of him," the young man told me. "You need to free him up. He'll still be around for you and his other loved ones in the future, but he'll also be tending to his further spiritual development. Right now, though, he's putting too much of his focus on his attachment to the earth plane. That's not good for him or any of you, either."

He continued to explain that Arthur's visits could help us with our grief because they showed us that we hadn't really lost him at all. Once we accepted that, our sadness wouldn't be as sharp and painful and Arthur could let go of the earth plane with greater ease.

My roommate's friend was right: I hadn't let go of my uncle at all. In fact, I thought of him every day. And although I was relatively tear free lately, during those first few months I had cried every day.

He was also right about the reassurance that Arthur's bathroom visit had brought me. I knew I had to begin letting go, and I did.

Because my relationship with my own father had always been strained, my uncle had come to symbolize the unconditional, consistent love and emotional security that my immediate family could not provide. I now had to realize that Arthur's love had not died when he did, that Arthur's concern, guidance, and support were still in my life even though his physical body had taken up residence in a different dimension. Intuitively, I would always have an open door to him, and that meant *sensing* his presence, and *feeling* conversations with him instead of actually having all of that in the physical realm with someone made of flesh and bone. As soon as I relaxed and trusted this intuitive process, my acceptance of his death became much easier and the bond with his spirit was cemented. I can feel his presence as a comfort, not a crutch, whenever I think of him.

A few months after the bathroom visit, I had the first of four dreams in which Arthur has made contact with me during the past sixteen years.

In the first dream—a classic example of the "I'm okay, you're okay" conversations that often take place among those who maintain contact—I found myself sitting on a park bench in an amusement park. The sun shone brightly; the air was clear; it wasn't too muggy or too dry; the temperature was just perfect. It felt like someone had ordered up the perfect late-spring day.

The amusement park was colorful and in pristine condition and completely deserted except for me.

Sitting on the bench, I knew I'd come there for a reason, I just didn't know what that reason was. That didn't trouble me in the least. I sat there calmly, peacefully, enjoying the gorgeous day.

I sat across from an intricately designed carousel whose horses were painted in shimmering pink, peach, and gold pastels. Suddenly, its music began—sweet, tinkly, playful— and the carousel started to revolve. I watched as the "horsies" (I thought of them having that name, as if seeing them triggered a childlike glee) passed at a moderate speed. Like the quality of the day, even the carousel was just right—not too fast, not too slow.

As the horses passed, riding up and down to the music, I watched, transfixed. Revolution after revolution, the horses played alone. There were no riders on any of them. So I was startled a bit then to see my uncle Arthur sitting on one of the horses as it rounded from the back side of the carousel and came into view.

Just as his horse got to the midpoint of the carousel, exactly opposite where I was sitting on the park bench, the carousel stopped spinning and, with a warm smile, my uncle Arthur climbed down from the horse onto the carousel's platform, then took one big step down to the ground.

I remained seated and watched, feeling a comforting, loving, soft glow around me. If the mood could have spoken it would have sighed, "Everything is just fine, all is well in the world."

Arthur walked toward me in a steady, even, almost flowing manner. Yet, there wasn't anything particularly ethereal about him, the amusement park, the carousel, or even me. It all seemed like a normal day, that is if a normal day is *very, very,* nice.

He sat down on the bench with me, to my right, and I turned to face him. We said little to each other aloud. Our thoughts were exchanged just by looking at each other. We sensed each other's feelings. When he did speak it was to simply tell me that he was okay, that he missed all of us, that we shouldn't worry about him. I told him how much we all loved him and missed him. His tone was reassuring and protective, yet not at all worried. Like everything else, it was *just right.* I told him a few brief tidbits about the family when he asked how everyone was. Then he told me that he would visit with me again, that he would periodically "check in." It was as if he wanted me to know that he really hadn't gone away for good, that while we might be seeing less of him than we had, he would be around from time to time to see how we were doing, to reassure us that he was fine.

With that, he got up from the park bench. Our good-byes were telepathic, not spoken. Then he turned, took a few steps, and simply vanished.

I knew that he would continue to watch over all of us. I knew that I was to share this dream visit with other members of my family in the same way you might mention a phone call from a faraway loved one. Then I woke up.

"Guess who I heard from," I'd begin each conversation when I told a few select family members and friends. Their response was as even as the dream—they weren't skeptical or overly excited, just a bit fascinated by my experience and pleased at Arthur's continued presence.

Gradually, over the years, I would learn that Arthur's wife, daughter, son-in-law, and daughter-in-law were having their own varied types of continued communication with him. As we shared stories we realized that he'd been in consistent contact since the day he died. Never more than a few months would pass without some impossible to ignore, dramatic contact with one of us. These contacts came in the form of dreams, synchronicities clearly tied to him, sensory experiences (like the smell of his pipe, or a gentle tap on the shoulder), a feeling of presence and guidance, hearing his voice, and even physical occurrences like the movement of objects.

Each one of us felt completely at ease with his continued presence in our lives.

My second dream came about a year after the first. In it, I was again alone. This time it was the backstage area of a large theater. Again, I knew I was there for a purpose, didn't know what it was, and wasn't bothered by not knowing. I walked past the huge ropes that opened and closed the stage's curtain. I walked past the gray concrete walls and out to the top of a very long hallway. Heading down the hallway, I saw dressing-room doors on my right, one after the other. The floor was gray concrete, the walls a nondescript color, the dressing-room doors the dark beige of old wood. It was a big, old, traditional theater, but nicely kept up. As I continued slowly down the extremely long hallway, I focused my eyes on the other end. Suddenly, my uncle Arthur appeared at the other end, simply standing quietly with his arms at his sides.

I continued walking. He began to walk. We met midway down the hall.

As in the carousel dream, we communicated our thoughts and feelings telepathically and again did not touch each other. He appeared quite solid, quite real. Except for the fact that he simply materialized out of nowhere, everything else about the scene was quite normal.

It was so *good* to see him again. Our verbal exchange was much like our conversation on the park bench in the previous dream. Again, he asked how I was, how the rest of the family was. I told him we were all fine, told him a few details, told him we missed him. Again, he reassured me that he was fine, that he loved and missed us, too, and that he'd be back once again to "check in" with me. We said our telepathic good-byes, and as in the previous dream, he turned, began to walk away, then simply disappeared.

I woke up.

During the next dozen or so years, while other family members were having their communications with Arthur, I continually felt his presence and would often speak aloud to him, the way someone might speak to a loved one at their grave during a cemetery visit. But, I have never visited his grave since the day of his funeral. I simply talk to him wherever I am, whenever I please, and I *know* that he hears me.

Within the last two years, Arthur has come to me in dreams twice more. One of the dreams is so vague that the only thing I remember is that he was in it, telepathically and verbally going through the usual "check in" routine, but with a little something extra this time. His energy was far more intense. I felt the comfort of his *spiritual* protection, his support, guidance, and love. When I woke up, I had the idea that I should specifically request him to make dream and other kinds of visits, that he would respond to my call for his company. I had never done any of that before. He'd just shown up in the past without my asking specifically for him to do so.

Not long after that dream, the feeling of his presence intensified, and I knew that I had made some kind of spiritual leap. I knew that he was as close and available to me as any friend, family member, or colleague I might seek out for anything from a fun chat to the sharing of news and information to brainstorming an idea to emotional support or advice. I knew that however he managed to do it, he was one of a number of guides who were keeping an eye on me and lending a hand when needed.

A few months ago, he appeared in a fourth dream. This time, I'd put out the spiritual equivalent of an A.P.B. for him. The sense that I had from this dream was that he was busy at the time with other things, but wanted me to know that he was available for me. This time we didn't have a private face-to-face meeting. Instead, I found myself in my aunt's walk-in closet, standing in front of a row of dresses and blouses. I looked down and saw Arthur's feet. He was wearing the same black dress shoes he'd always worn. He was hiding behind my aunt's clothes! All I could see of him was from the midcalves down. Briefly, I caught a glimpse of the rest of him, in shadow, behind the clothes. He stayed behind them while we had a quick visit. Our communication was mostly telepathic. We dispensed with the "check in" portion of our usual visits, and got right down to business. I told him, mostly telepathically, but some of it verbally, why I had called for him. He gave me the up-front, honest feedback that had always been his trademark both in his life before he passed on and after. He was also filled with love, reassurance, and positive energy. He didn't try to rush me out of there, but I sensed that it was time for me to go, that he was in his wife's closet as part of his continuing guidance for her, and that he'd "squeezed me into his schedule," much as a doctor does when you have an emergency and he has a full load of patients coming in that day. I knew that Arthur was happy to squeeze me into his spiritual schedule, and having completed what I came into the closet to do, I said a cheery good-bye and left.

Then I woke up.

It comes naturally to me to regard Arthur as one of my spiritual guides. He keeps proving he is over and over. I'm not the only one he guides, of course, but like the good father, uncle, brother, friend, and businessman that he was before he passed on, he takes the time now to continue to make a difference in everyone's life.

Very recently I learned the extent of his communication with his daughter-in-law, Diane, the wife of his oldest son.

On a spring day in 1978, Diane was going over a list of baby names. She and her husband had just been told that a baby had been born, but they weren't told the baby's sex. They were next "in line" for the adoption process, and this baby would come to live with them in three months, according to the state law at the time. Diane really liked the name Arianne. In keeping with the Jewish tradition of naming the baby after a loved one who has passed on, either using the exact name or one that begins with the same letter, Diane realized that even though she liked the name Arianne so much, there wasn't a deceased relative or friend whose name began with an A whom she could honor in this manner. She wouldn't necessarily even have to match the first letter of a deceased one's name, though, she remembered; she could honor them by giving the baby the deceased one's Hebrew name regardless of either of their English names. A Hebrew name is given in a baby-naming ceremony at the synagogue if the baby is a girl, and during the *bris,* the circumcision ceremony, if the baby is a boy. Still, she thought about whether she'd overlooked someone in the family who had passed on whose name began with A, and, coming up empty, realized that one person in the family whose name began with an A, and whom she loved very much, was Arthur, her father-in-law. But Arthur was not deceased, and so the baby could not be named in his memory.

Sometime later that day—she doesn't remember exactly how much time passed between her thinking about this and when the phone rang—she got the call informing her that Arthur had died on the golf course. He'd probably passed on just as she was thinking about wanting to name the baby after someone in the family whose name began with an A. Her first reaction, she says now quietly, was of being spooked, as if somehow her thoughts about baby's names led to Arthur suddenly being available for the honor. Then she quickly realized that she had it backwards. It was Arthur's passing that triggered Diane's thoughts about the letter A and how Arthur couldn't be a candidate for the honor. Arthur's spirit, she knew, had signaled her when he died.

Diane had not told anyone in the family that a baby was finally available, and she felt guilty that Arthur passed away not knowing that his grandchild would be joining the family. After Arthur's death, she told the family about the baby. They later learned that it was a boy, and named him Allen, after Arthur.

Beginning a few months later, Diane began having yearly dreams in which Arthur would come to spend a day with her family. In the first one, she told him about the baby, and he told her that he already knew about him. She took him upstairs to the baby's nursery to introduce them. During this first visit, Arthur explained to Diane, her husband, their two children, and Arthur's widow that he would be allowed to come spend a day with them once a year, but that at the end of the evening he would have to leave. They shouldn't be sad, though, he told them, because he would be back for another such family day the following year.

Each year, the basics of Diane's dream are the same:

Arthur, dressed in a short-sleeved shirt and casual pants, appearing to be the age he was when he passed on, is brought to Diane's home by his wife. In the years since his widow remarried, her second husband, Marvin, is present for these visits and Arthur is comfortable with that, as is everyone else. They all sit in the living room for a visit, tell Arthur what's new—he always says he already knows!— talk over things with him, get his advice, the usual family conversation. Everyone treats him as if he's "alive," Diane says. They can all touch him. Yet they know that he lives on the other side now, and that he's not "alive" in the same sense.

They then go into the dining room for dinner, and he stays for a few hours more, before announcing that it's time to go. His wife always escorts him out the front door when he has to leave.

Diane says the timing of these visits is interesting: they usually occur around the time of a special occasion, like the wedding of Arthur's grandson last year. During Diane's dream, they told him about the wedding, and he told them that he was there, in spirit, "standing" next to the bride and groom.

In these dreams, no matter what time of year they actually occur, it's never winter, and Arthur always shows up in short-sleeved shirts. She wonders if that's because he passed away in the spring.

"It's the most comforting, pleasant feeling," Diane says. "And he always eats dinner with us. When we're gathered at my house, we're all expecting him, it's not a shock, except for the first dream, when we were very surprised to see him walk in. The whole thing feels very natural. Each visit picks up where the last one ended. We are all thrilled to see him."

During one dream, years ago, "Arthur walked through the house and said how much he liked what we did with it," she says, laughing. He had died before they decorated and got settled in.

"We talk more than he does. He nods a lot and is very reassuring," Diane tells me. "And each time he reminds me that he can only stay for a day. During the first dream when he told me that I cried before he left, but I don't anymore in the dreams because I know he'll be back."

When Diane told me about these dreams, I admit I was a bit envious, because Arthur's visits with them last a whole day in her dreams, and my visits with him are so much shorter. But then I figured that it made sense. When he goes to their house, of course he'll stay a full day—this is his immediate family (or at least part of it)—his oldest son, daughter-in-law, grandchildren, and his wife. Not knowing that such a long visit was possible until Diane mentioned the dreams, I told her I thought that we should all put in our official request for a full day with Arthur and see what happened.

I wonder if he'll be able to show up in dreams for his daughter and his other son or any of the rest of the family.

Arthur has a unique, consistent, and long-running relationship from the afterlife with his daughter's husband, who was his business partner. He has continued to advise his son-in-law about business matters, but not in dreams.

"I was awake," Ron tells me. "I don't want to believe it

but I *know* he was there. The last time was about a year ago. I've tried to make it go away."

It's not surprising that the three people whom Arthur has chosen to communicate with in the most vivid ways—his daughter-in-law, his son-in-law, and me—are all extremely intuitive people who have always been open and highly sensitive to all things spiritual or metaphysical. Having said that, it's also interesting to note how Ron has reacted to contact. He knows it's happening, yet this "proof" leaves him feeling astounded. He's an inventor and an engineer, with a trained scientific mind. He'd like very much to have his dispassionate, logical side rule out the possibility of interdimensional communication. On the other hand, he knows that even science shows that energy dynamics make this kind of contact something that one cannot flatly rule out.

I joked with him that he must be feeling what people felt years ago upon first learning that the world was round and not flat. They could hardly deny the truth, but it took some getting used to.

Ron's experiences have been so clear that the truth of them can be reconciled by the part of him that is spiritually and metaphysically educated. He knows that it is all real.

"Ninety percent of the time it would happen at work," Ron says. "I'd sense him near me, out of the corner of my eye. I'd be working on something and then have this sense that I'd been 'told' something about it, something that would help with the project. I'd put this new idea off for a day or two, because I wasn't sure where it came from. It didn't feel like it came from *me*. And, as if to remind me to pay attention to this new idea, I'd see all kinds of stuff out of place at the office, like it had been moved. It was like Arthur was trying to get my attention. These ideas had come from *him*. And they ended up always working."

Arthur came around the most after he'd first passed away.

"I had so much of his business and personal financial stuff to wrap up," Ron says. "I had quite a lot to deal with, and it was often frustrating, and I would stand alone in a room and talk out loud to him, not really seriously thinking he could hear me, but I'd ask him a question. Well, in a day or so I'd have an answer. And it was like he was always leading me to things. I'd find documents that we couldn't locate before, but through a series of coincidences, or synchronicities, I now believe he orchestrated I'd find what we needed. At first I wanted to write it off as dumb luck, or call it coincidence, but I've always really known better. I know that there's no such thing as a coincidence. It all comes from *somewhere,* and in this case it was coming from Arthur."

In one such case, Ron closed the door to his private office in their electronics plant building, and it locked. The keys, he realized, were inside the office. It was five-thirty, so he went home thinking, "What would Arthur have done if he locked himself out of his office?"

After dinner, Ron's wife (Arthur's daughter), casually handed him an envelope with dozens of old photos inside, photos taken when Arthur was alive. Looking through them, he noticed a photo of Arthur standing in front of his own office door. Ron thought this rather coincidental. He'd never seen the photo before and wondered why it had been taken.

"I thought something looked funny about the photo," he says. "And then I noticed that one of Arthur's pants cuffs is caught on something and rolled up a bit. Looking at that made me notice the carpet he was standing on, and that reminded me that years ago when it was safe for people to do this kind of thing there was always a spare key under the mat at the front door to Arthur's house. I thought maybe he'd hidden a spare key to my office door under the carpeting in front of it."

The next morning, Ron went into work, peeled back the edge of the carpeting in front of his office door, and found a spare key.

After Ron recounted this and a few other stories, we discussed how energy passes interdimensionally. We talked about how even the most skeptical scientists, when faced with the validation of their own experiences, realize that there is *something going on here.* This discussion took place on the phone; Ron was on the upstairs extension in his house. In the midst of a joking moment of skepticism, in which Ron admitted how much he believed in afterlife communication while at the same time hating the idea of having to admit it, his wife called out to him from downstairs in the kitchen: "Did you get the phone?"

"What are you talking about?" Ron asked her. "I'm already on the phone, I've been talking to Julie for an hour."

"You two are still on the phone?" She had picked up the kitchen extension and said this to both of us on the phone. "I'd thought you hung up. This is impossible."

"What are you talking about?" Ron asked her.

"The phone rang three times," she said, "and I was busy in the other room, couldn't get to it, and I was calling out for you to answer it. I guess you didn't hear me. I didn't know you were upstairs."

"The phone couldn't have rung," Ron said. "I'm *on* it. I've been on it for an hour."

"It did ring," she insisted. "It rang at least three times, then stopped."

After she hung up, Ron sighed and I laughed.

"Why are you laughing?" he asked me, even though I was sure he already knew the answer.

"Why are you sighing?" I asked, wanting to know what was on his mind before I told him why I was laughing.

"Because just before she yelled up here asking if I had picked up the phone, just at the time she obviously heard it ringing, I felt some kind of energy pulse on the phone and wondered what in the world it was."

I then told him why I was laughing, and it was exactly why he was sighing. We both knew that the phone ringing had been a sign from Arthur, his way of saying to us, "Why are you two discussing the energy possibilities and wondering if it's really what's occurring or just a theory? *I'll show you possibilities* . . . I'm gonna make the phone ring while you're already on it."

Somehow, that's exactly what Arthur managed to do, bless his soul!

Epilogue

Death doesn't bother me a bit. It's got to be interesting. There's no way I'm just lying there. Something is gonna happen!

JERRY SEINFELD

Western culture tends to make death a very serious, somber, sad turn of events. Think about the phrases we use: "deadly serious," "scared to death," "dead wrong." When was the last time you heard someone here say "deadly happy," or "joyful to death," or use the term death in anything but a negative and often gruesome way?

We associate death with the negative from a physical standpoint because the illnesses, accidents, and injuries that lead to the loss of physical life are so often accompanied by great pain and suffering. Our fear of death comes from our fear of having to go through intense pain. Our fear of death comes also from assuming, incorrectly, that it is the end of our minds,

149

spirits, souls, personalities, beings—whatever you want to call our human essence—simply because it is the end of our physical bodies. We can't and don't want to conceive of *not existing*.

Ironic, then, that many have a hard time believing we *do* continue to exist after death, our mind intact within our spirit. We have a hard time believing this because Western culture and society has a hard time picturing a mind/spirit/soul that can exist apart from its physical body. Once we get beyond that artificial hurdle, accepting that life goes on after death is natural and easy.

Think about the phrase "at death's door" and you'll understand that death isn't an end, it's an entryway to the next phase of life, a phase lived in a higher-vibrational dimension.

Death itself is not negative or painful. Death itself is a release of the spirit from the physical restrictions of the human body it has been inhabiting. Death is a homecoming for the soul, a return to its natural state as a nonphysical spiritual being, in its natural home in the higher-dimensional realm. The soul came to the earthly plane only in order to go to school. Think of the human body as the school's uniform. When you go home, you change out of your uniform into something more comfortable. At home your education continues; so do love, play, leisure, family and friendship relationships, passion, spiritual enlightenment, compassion, service to others, personal growth, and communication.

When a soul goes "home" to the higher-dimensional realm it can and does keep in touch with those of us still at the earthly plane school. We have only but to recognize its language.

Bibliography

Armstrong, Karen. *A History of God.* New York: Ballantine Books, 1994.

Becker, Ernest. *The Denial of Death.* New York: The Free Press/Macmillan, 1973.

Ben Shlomo, Rabbi Eliyahu. "Life After Death and the World to Come." *Return to the Source: Selected Articles on Judaism and Teshuva.* New York: Feldheim Publishing, 1984.

Brinkley, Dannion. *Saved by the Light.* New York: Villard Books, 1994.

Durant, Will. *The Story of Philosophy.* New York: Pocket Books/ Simon & Schuster, 1961.

Editors of Time-Life Books. *Search for the Soul.* New York: Time-Life Books, 1989.

Evans-Wentz, W. Y. *The Tibetan Book of the Dead.* Third Edition. New York: Oxford University Press, 1960.

Haynes, C. B. *When a Man Dies*. Washington, D.C.: Review and Herald Publishing Association, 1948.

Jacobs, Louis. *Hasidic Thought*. Behrman House, 1976.

Kaku, Michio. *Hyperspace*. New York: Oxford University Press, 1994.

Martin, Joel, and Romanowski, Patricia. *We Don't Die: George Anderson's Conversations with the Other Side*. New York: Berkley Books, 1989.

Medicine Eagle, Brooke. *Buffalo Woman Comes Singing*. New York: Ballantine, 1991.

Monroe, Robert A. *Ultimate Journey*. New York: Doubleday, 1994.

Moody, Raymond A., Jr. *Life After Life*. New York: Bantam Books, 1976.

Nau, Erika S. *Huna Self-Awareness: Hawaii's Ancient Wisdom*. York Beach, Maine: Samuel Weiser, Inc., 1992.

Pliskin, Rabbi Zelig. *Consulting the Wise*. New York: Benei Yakov Publishing, 1991.

Redfield, James. *The Celestine Prophecy*. New York: Warner Books, 1993.

Tedlock, Dennis, and Tedlock, Barbara. *Teachings from the American Earth*. New York: Liveright, 1992.

Thoreau, Henry David. *Walden*. New York: New American Library, 1960.

Bibliography

Tooker, Elizabeth. *Native North American Spirituality of the Eastern Woodlands*. Mahwah, N.J.: Paulist Press, 1979.

Viney, Geoff. *Surviving Death: Evidence of the Afterlife*. New York: St. Martin's Press, 1994.

Whitton, Joel L., and Fisher, Joe. *Life Between Life*. New York: Warner Books, 1988.

Wolf, Fred Alan. *The Eagle's Quest: A Physicist's Search for Truth in the Heart of the Shamanic World*. New York: Touchstone Books/Simon & Schuster, 1990.